MW00720245

To Larry.

the
BEST
LOVED
BOAT

Bon Voyage

Ian Kennedy

the
BEST
LOVED
BOAT

The *Princess Maquinna*

IAN KENNEDY

HARBOUR
PUBLISHING

Harbour Publishing Co. Ltd.
P.O. Box 219, Madeira Park, BC, V0N 2H0
www.harbourpublishing.com

Copy edited by Jonathan Dore
Indexed by Colleen Bidner
Cover and text design by Setareh Ashrafologhalai
Printed and bound in Canada
Author photo by Terry Pargee
Front cover image courtesy of the Royal BC Museum
Back cover photo by Harold Monks, courtesy of Lois Warner

Harbour Publishing acknowledges the support of the Canada
Council for the Arts, the Government of Canada and the Province
of British Columbia through the BC Arts Council.

Library and Archives Canada Cataloguing in Publication

Title: The best loved boat :
The Princess Maquinna / Ian Kennedy.
Names: Kennedy, Ian, 1943- author.
Description: Includes bibliographical references and index.
Identifiers: Canadiana (print) 20230473792 | Canadiana (ebook)
20230473954 | ISBN 9781990776403
(hardcover) | ISBN 9781990776410 (EPUB)
Subjects: LCSH: Princess Maquinna (Ship) |
LCSH: Vancouver Island (B.C.)—History.
Classification: LCC FC3844 .K46 2023 | DDC 971.1/2—dc23

For my dear wife Judith
(1949–2020)

CONTENTS

MAP viii

INTRODUCTION 1

CHAPTER 1   **CASTING OFF**   7

CHAPTER 2   **BC BUILT**   19

CHAPTER 3   **FIRST STOP**   31

CHAPTER 4   **THE TRAIL**   39

CHAPTER 5   **BOAT LANDINGS**   45

CHAPTER 6   **SEEING THE SIGHTS**   57

CHAPTER 7   **BAMFIELD**   69

CHAPTER 8   **SHELTERED WATERS**   77

CHAPTER 9   **BARKLEY SOUND**   87

CHAPTER 10   **SHIPWRECK AND SAFE HARBOUR**   97

CHAPTER 11   **CLAYOQUOT SOUND**   111

CHAPTER 12   **HESQUIAHT AND ESTEVAN**   125

CHAPTER 13   **NOOTKA SOUND**   133

CHAPTER 14   **ZEBALLOS AND ESPERANZA**   145

CHAPTER 15   **QUATSINO SOUND**   155

CHAPTER 16   **HEADING SOUTH**   169

CHAPTER 17   **TOURISM AND TRAGEDY**   177

CHAPTER 18   **WARTIME ON THE WEST COAST**   189

CHAPTER 19   **THE FINAL YEARS**   199

CHAPTER 20   **TRIBUTES**   211

ACKNOWLEDGEMENTS   217

NOTES   219

BIBLIOGRAPHY   229

INDEX   235

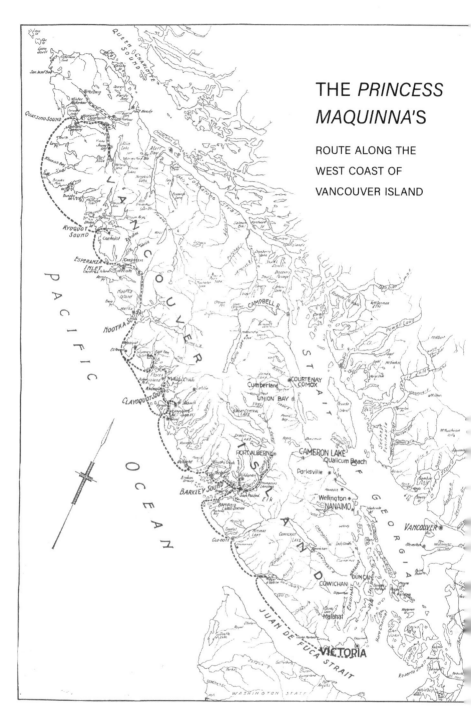

THE *PRINCESS MAQUINNA'S*

ROUTE ALONG THE
WEST COAST OF
VANCOUVER ISLAND

A section of a Canadian Pacific Railway tourist brochure map. IMAGE FROM
93-7330 EARL MARSH ACCESSION BOX 22, COURTESY OF THE ROYAL BC MUSEUM.

INTRODUCTION

I N THE EARLY 1920S, people seeking adventure and a unique travel experience could take a cruise up and down the west coast of Vancouver Island on the "Good Ship" SS *Princess Maquinna,* visiting dozens of stops on the steamer's regular run from Victoria to the north end of the island and back again. This ship, built in Esquimalt, one of a fleet of nineteen *Princess* ships owned and operated by the Canadian Pacific Steamship Company (CPSC, part of the global Canadian Pacific Railway empire), had been in service since 1913. In her early years the *Maquinna* catered mainly to west coast locals living or working at many far-flung, remote locations along the coast. A decade later, however, the owners recognizedthe need people had for recreation and enjoyment, and began trumpeting the many attractions of the ship and the wild, west coast of Vancouver Island.

Imagine being a tourist stepping aboard the SS *Princess Maquinna* in the summer of 1924, looking forward to an unforgettable, week-long voyage of some 770 nautical miles (1,420 km) up and down the rugged west coast of Vancouver Island. The Canadian Pacific brochures boasted that passengers would view magnificent scenery; eat scrumptious meals in the ship's elegant dining room (perhaps even at the captain's table); sleep in comfortable, well-appointed cabins; play deck games such as quoits and shuffleboard on the upper deck; and meet interesting fellow passengers, many from west coast communities. The enticements on offer included tourists being able to interact with the friendly captain, officers and crew and learn from them about the ship and about the west coast. They might learn how the ship could travel in fog and still keep to her timetable; how the ship, captain and crew coped with wild winter storms; interested passengers might even be invited down to the engine room to see how the vessel's triple expansion steam engine worked.

In good weather, passengers could step out on deck and see all sorts of wildlife: whales, seals, sea lions, Pacific white-sided dolphins and hundreds of varieties of birds, including bald eagles. When the ship stopped at some ports of call, passengers could disembark and take tours of local communities, fish canneries, logging camps and whaling stations.

Along the way, passengers would likely encounter Nuu-cha-nulth First Nations people who had lived along Vancouver Island's west coast for thousands of years. CP brochures depict magnificent totem poles that passengers would see, and mention how passengers could buy keepsakes such as woven baskets and carvings from Indigenous women selling their handicrafts at various stops along the way. Passengers could take time at Friendly Cove to wander through the haunting graveyard, with its assortment of "tokens of remembrances" enhancing the stockade-like enclosures around some of the graves. In Quatsino Sound, voyagers might encounter some of the few remaining Indigenous women with flattened heads, the result of shaping infants' foreheads, by strapping on boards.

Passengers booking passage for a trip on the SS *Princess Maquinna* in 1924 would know that the ship regularly leaves Victoria harbour at 11 p.m., three times a month, proceeding from there along the Strait of Juan de Fuca until, in the early morning, she arrives at her first port of call, Port Renfrew, a small logging and fishing community. After a short stop, an hour's sail brings the vessel to Clo-oose, one of the most interesting calls of the entire journey, located on a particularly treacherous stretch of the coastline known as the Graveyard of the Pacific. Here, as there is no dock, Ditidaht men and women paddle out from shore in their dugout canoes to the freight doors at the side of the ship and load goods and people into their canoes, carrying them ashore through the heavy surf. Dunkings could occur in rough weather, adding to the excitement.

Shortly after leaving Clo-oose, located on the West Coast Lifesaving Trail—created to provide shipwrecked sailors a lifeline on this dangerous coast—the ship turns in to Bamfield, tying up at the dock overlooked by the imperial government cable station. This relay station is on the "All Red Line" cable telegraph network, a global network running only through British imperial territories. It began operations in 1902, relaying messages from Australia and New Zealand across the Pacific, transferring them across Canada and on to Great Britain. Passengers have time to visit the palatial station and talk with some of the young—mostly Australian—men working the telegraph keys.

From Bamfield, the steamship sails up the 30-mile (50-km) Alberni Canal to Port Alberni, stopping along the way at a variety of fish-packing plants where large quantities of herring and pilchard are rendered into fish oil and meal. After sailing back along this narrow stretch of water, the *Maquinna* turns north across Barkley Sound, through the Broken Islands, making a stop at Sechart, one of three whaling stations on the trip. If passengers can stand the stench, they watch workers render whales into oil, meat and meal, and perhaps pick up a whale tooth or a piece of baleen or bone as a souvenir. Later, at Ucluelet, a treat awaits those passengers with a green thumb. Here George Fraser's magical garden awaits, where he raises plants and seeds for shipment the world over. So renowned is Fraser that a rhododendron bearing his name still grows in Kew Gardens in London. Not interested in gardens? Take an excursion, run by a local family, to go and see the most stunning strand in all of Canada, Long Beach. Eight miles (13 km) long, used by the locals as part of the rough roadway between Ucluelet and Tofino, the beach is a wondrous sight.

Three hours steaming from Ucluelet brings the ship into Clayoquot Sound, where she makes calls at the growing village of Tofino, and at Clayoquot, on Stubbs Island, set on a lovely sandy spit with a long curving dock topped with rails for its freight trolley. Leaving Clayoquot, the ship sails north, up the protected waters of the sound, to Kakawis, the large Roman Catholic Indian Mission School, and from there to the village of Ahousaht, on Flores Island.

Two hours after rounding Estevan Point, at the north end of Clayoquot Sound, the *Maquinna* arrives at historic Nootka Sound, where Captain James Cook landed in 1778. Friendly Cove, as Cook called the harbour, possesses a dramatic collection of totem poles; here passengers may learn how, a decade after Cook's visit, a confrontation in this isolated community almost led to a war halfway around the globe, between Spain and Great Britain.

After leaving Nootka Sound the *Maquinna* steams north into Esperanza Inlet and Kyuquot Sound, where she makes a variety of stops at remote logging camps, reduction plants, various mines and at another whaling station, Cachalot. Everywhere she stops, the ship drops off mail, passengers and foodstuffs, as well as needed industrial supplies, while picking up passengers and local products for shipment to Victoria and beyond.

After rounding Brooks Peninsula—which sticks out of the west side of Vancouver Island like a thumb—the *Maquinna* enters the protected waters of Quatsino Sound, where she makes several stops, the most important at the pulp and paper mill at Port Alice. Finally, at Holberg, she makes her final stop on the northern leg of her journey, 385 nautical miles (710 km) from Victoria.

Turning south, the *Maquinna* stops at various ports of call to pick up passengers and freight on her way back to Victoria. There, passengers disembark in the inner harbour early in the morning, seven days after setting out on a trip that will surely live in their memories for years to come, and perhaps will tempt many to return for another voyage sometime in the future.

For over four decades, the faithful *Princess Maquinna* repeated this lengthy trip up and down the west coast countless times. Some of her trips were shorter, turning back to Victoria from Nootka or other way ports, but she never flagged, never quit. She steamed back and forth in summer and winter, in calm and storm, in war and in peace, creating for herself a legendary status, and becoming the best-loved boat in BC's maritime history.

This is her remarkable story.

CHAPTER 1

CASTING OFF

I N THE SUMMER of 1924, as the 11 p.m. departure time of the ss *Princess Maquinna* nears, the new and imposing Canadian Pacific Steamship terminal on Belleville Street in Victoria bustles with activity. Locally known as the "Temple of Poseidon," and designed, like the nearby Empress Hotel and British Columbia Legislative Building, by noted architect Francis Rattenbury, the terminus had opened just weeks before. Taxis roll up and streetcars disgorge fares, as others walk to the terminal carrying bags and belongings. Businessmen, loggers, cannery workers, mothers carrying newborn babies, families, priests in cassocks and nuns in habits, First Nations folk and tourists all make their way inside to the ticket office. Everyone is heading up the coast aboard the ship, sometimes referred to as the "Ugly Duckling" or the "Ugly Princess" but most often, and lovingly, called "Old Reliable" or "Old Faithful." During her seven-day voyage up and down Vancouver Island's rugged and dangerous west coast, the *Maquinna* will stop at up to forty ports of call. Those with means buy first-class berths in one of the ship's fifty staterooms; others choose the less expensive second-class option, which has them sharing a four-bunk cabin with fellow passengers; others simply opt to sit in the ship's main lounge for the trip. "Indians and Orientals"—as they are called in the CP fare schedule at this time—pay half the first-class fare, but are forced to remain outside on the forward deck.

The Canadian Pacific Railway's marine terminal
at Belleville Street, Victoria. Designed by P. Leonard James and Francis
Mawson Rattenbury. IMAGE D-05216 COURTESY OF THE ROYAL BC MUSEUM.

With tickets in hand, the passengers, some accompanied by friends who have come to see them off, walk through the ticket office and make their way onto the ship to be greeted by ship's officers, stewards and stewardesses. As the passengers board, stevedores and the ship's crew load mountains of freight into the *Maquinna*'s three cargo holds—two forward, one aft. Some of that cargo, such as wooden boxes full of groceries, sides of beef, fruit, vegetables, bits of machinery, furniture, construction material, coils of rope and wire and empty wooden barrels, the crew load through the 2-metre-high by 2.5-metre-wide (6′ 2″ by 8′ 9″) cargo doors set in the ship's side. Inside the hold, the deck hands and the ship's purser, clipboard in hand, sort the tons of goods, moving the various items around the cargo deck using solidly built Fairbanks-Morse railway dollies and stout ropes to secure various items to ringbolts set into the hold's sides. The crew places all cargo so it will come out at the various ports of call in the reverse order to which they loaded it, following the maxim "first on, last off." Amid all the hustle and bustle, dogs, tied up in the forward hold, bark and howl, adding to the cacophony. On the forward outer deck, larger and more awkward items, such as lumber, large pieces of machinery, engines, oil, gasoline and kerosene drums, bales of hay, cows and horses, sometimes even an automobile, are lifted from the dock using the ship's derricks, capable of lifting eight tons. Special hooks and slings come into play to lift awkward items using the ship's three pairs of steam winches, manned by long-time expert winchman "Shorty" Wright. Johnnie Vanden Wouwer, of Bamfield, recalled that once "They took a troller [a fishboat] up on the bow deck; a thirty foot troller for Kyuquot!"[1] Back inside, the purser stores the more precious cargo such as mail, small parcels and fragile goods under lock and key in the special mailroom, located near the bow inside the forward cargo hold.

From the moment passengers come aboard the ss *Princess Maquinna*, the ship's layout encourages them to mingle with their fellow passengers and the ship's crew. "There wasn't anywhere to go, everyone had to be friendly."[2]

When entering the ship, they step into a space serving as the ship's lobby, a gathering place with couchettes of green leather built around the walls. Here, those who do not have cabins will spend the journey. The lounge also holds the newsstand, selling newspapers and confectionaries, as well as a ticket office, where those who board the ship at various ports of call after it leaves Victoria will pay their fares. An upright piano also stands in the lounge ready for those who can play to entertain their fellow passengers. Often impromptu singsongs and dances break out. This ship's lounge represents the main congregating area for the voyage, but people also gather in the nearby smoking room and in the dining room, just down a passageway. Travelling on the *Maquinna* is akin to boarding a local bus. People know each other because the west coast communities from which many of them come are so small that most everyone knows everyone everywhere, if they are local. Familiar faces are not hard to find. Victoria's *Daily Colonist* regularly reports on the ship's arrivals and departures, what cargoes she carries, and also lists most of the passengers who travel on her. Here is a typical passenger list from November 2, 1913:

> When *Maquinna* slipped away from the Belleville Street wharves last night she was again in command of Capt. Gillam. Among passengers who sailed were: H. Baines, G. Davis, Mrs. William Clancy, H.B. Round, F.V. Longstaff, H. Mahoney, C.B. Whaley, W.S. Taylor, Robert Wallace, M. McDonald, J. Hogan, W. Jones, William Marshall, G. Tucker, C. Tucker, A. Haywood, M. Parnwill, L. Duckett, A. Luckovich, R.C. Lumsden, A. Johnson, Mrs. F. Baker, Mrs. G. Baker, J.C. Wright, Mr./Mrs. Bridger, Mr. Halkett.[3]

Once aboard, passengers with cabin bookings search the labyrinth of passageways for their cabins, and, if unfamiliar with the ship's layout, one of the ship's stewards or stewardesses will help direct the way. First-class passengers seek out the fifty staterooms, while second-class ticket holders share cabins on a lower deck. If all the cabins have been booked, second-class passengers sit in the lounge for the trip, while First Nations and Chinese or Japanese travellers, with their "deck class" tickets, remain outside on the forward deck, sometimes creating makeshift shelters under the companionways in bad weather. If the weather turns particularly foul, the captain might allow them to shelter in the forward cargo hold.

Five minutes before 11 p.m. a bell warns visitors that they should depart. At precisely 11 p.m. the ship's distinctive whistle sounds and, on the bridge, Captain Edward Gillam, the experienced ship's master, orders the hawsers to be let go and directs his helmsman to begin easing the *Maquinna* out into the confines of Victoria's tightly enclosed inner harbour. Captain Gillam knows Victoria Harbour and the west coast as well as anyone. He arrived on the west coast from George's Bay, Newfoundland, in 1879 at age 16. At first he sailed on sealing schooners but later became a deckhand on the ss *Queen City*, rising to become its master before becoming captain of the ss *Tees*. Familiar with the *Maquinna*'s sharp whistle and knowing its significance, many Victorians in their houses in Fairfield and James Bay knowingly announce to whoever is within hearing: "There goes the *Princess Maquinna*!"

Years of experience tell Captain Gillam exactly at what compass point he should order his helmsman to set the rudder, and for exactly how many minutes and seconds at a certain number of propeller revolutions the ship needs to back away from the dock. When the ship reaches that precise point in the constricted harbour, the helmsman changes course and the *Maquinna*'s bow slowly turns, aiming for the narrow gap between Laurel and Songhees Points. Once through the gap and out of the inner harbour, Gillam signals the engine room to increase steam and the ship picks up pace, heading toward more open waters. In order to run the ship Captain Gillam has four officers and sixteen ratings employed in the Deck Department, three in the Pursers' Department, three engineers and eight ratings in the Engine Room Department, three stewards/stewardesses, twelve waiters and bus boys, and five cooks—all Chinese—in the Stewards' Department. For managing this crew of fifty-four, keeping his vessel running efficiently and having the health, safety and welfare of his passengers resting on his broad shoulders, Captain Gillam earns the princely sum of $250 per month.

Once through the Laurel/Songhees Point gap, the *Maquinna* passes out of the harbour and past Fisgard Lighthouse, off its starboard bow. Built in 1890, British Columbia's oldest lighthouse stands at the entrance to Esquimalt Harbour. Twelve years earlier, inside that same harbour, the ss *Princess Maquinna* first came down the ways of the BC Marine Railway Company shipyard, on Christmas Eve 1912. In 1913, soon after the launch, the BC Marine Railway Company, then known familiarly as Bullen's yard, became Yarrows Shipyard. The construction and launch of the *Princess Maquinna* marked a hugely progressive step in the history of shipbuilding in

Captain Gillam with *Princess Maquinna*'s officers and the ship's nurse September 1916. *Back row, far left:* Norman Taylor; *far right:* Officer Kennedy. Captain Gillam is seated in the centre, next to the nurse. *Front row, left:* Second Officer Leonard Thompson; *right:* Assistant Purser D.E. Horner. IMAGE REV1 COURTESY OF THE VANCOUVER MARITIME MUSEUM.

British Columbia, particularly on the west coast of Vancouver Island, where strong, reliable ships had been in demand ever since the establishment of Fort Victoria by the Hudson's Bay Company back in 1843.

Back in the 1840s and 1850s, sailing schooners primarily served the seaborne transportation needs of the earliest trading posts on the west coast of Vancouver Island. In 1874, thirty years after the establishment of Fort Victoria, only four traders lived permanently on Vancouver Island's west coast: Fred Thornberg at Clayoquot, Peter Francis at Spring Cove in Ucluelet, Andrew Laing at Dodger's Cove in Barkley Sound and Neils Moos at Port San Juan. When settlement did eventually occur on the outer coast in the 1880s and 1890s, in places such as Port Alberni, Ucluelet, Clayoquot and Quatsino, the need arose for a reliable, regularly scheduled shipping service to serve the growing population and industries. Into that breach, in 1883, stepped the Canadian Pacific Navigation Company (CPNC).

Steam-driven vessels, such as the ones the CPNC used, arrived in British Columbia fifty years earlier when, in 1836, the Hudson's Bay Company contracted the Green, Wigram and Green shipyard at Blackwall, near London, to build the SS *Beaver* to serve the needs of the company. Two modest 35-horsepower engines powered her side paddles and drove the 102-ft (31-m) *Beaver* through BC waters for the next fifty-two years. She faithfully served as a freighter, tow-boat and even gun ship, eventually running aground near Stanley Park's Prospect Point, near the entrance to Vancouver Harbour, in 1888.[4] This modest beginning of steam-driven ships in BC led, in 1883, to the Hudson's Bay Company combining its then four vessels—the *Beaver, Otter, Enterprise* and *Princess Louise*—with the Pioneer Line, which had dominated the river steamboating business, mainly on the Fraser River, for over twenty years. This amalgamation formed the Canadian Pacific Navigation Company Ltd., with the Pioneer Line bringing its four steamers (mostly paddlewheelers)—the *R.P. Rithet, Western Slope, William Irving* and *Reliance*—into the new partnership. Optimism soared within the new CPNC because of the impending extension of the Canadian Pacific's transcontinental railway to Burrard Inlet, which surely would bring a huge increase in business, even though the CPNC, despite its name, had no financial connection to the Canadian Pacific Railway Company.

Within five years, the CPNC had established regular scheduled routes in the Strait of Georgia, the Fraser River and to northern ports on the mainland coast. Then in 1888 the company established its first bi-monthly service on the west coast of Vancouver Island when its SS *Maude* began a regular run from Victoria to Port Alberni and Barkley Sound. Originally a sidewheeler of only 113.5 ft (34.6 m) in length and 214 tons, this wooden-hulled vessel had been built on

San Juan Island and had her 150-horsepower engine installed in Victoria in 1872. In 1884, a refit removed her engine and she became a coal barge, but a year later, with a new engine installed, she became a propeller-driven screw steamer powered by a compound two-cylinder engine.

For a number of years, the *Maude* made her bi-monthly trips up and down the west coast of Vancouver Island, and by 1896, three trips a month. In 1895, however, with more mining activity in Barkley Sound, the little *Maude* proved inadequate to handle the growing trade, prompting the CPNC directors to purchase the ss *Tees* in 1896 to supplement and eventually to replace the *Maude*.

"The steamer *Tees,* which has been purchased (for $52,031.57) by the CPCN Co. to put on the west of Vancouver Island coast route, is a modern ship being thoroughly up to date in the matter of appointments, fixtures and machinery," declared the *Daily Colonist.* "Built at Stockton-on-Tees in 1893 she is 679 tons . . . Her dimensions are given as: length, 165 feet, beam 26 feet, depth of hold 10.8 feet. The vessel's machinery is also of the most modern description and capable of driving the vessel at a rate of 10½ knots. The engines are triple expansion, 95 [nominal] hp [horsepower] and last but not least . . . it includes an electric plant which lights the ship throughout." Built of steel with a double hull, she could accommodate seventy-five or more people in "spacious cabin accommodation."[5]

The *Tees* barely had time to make her inaugural run to Port Alberni in 1896 when news of the discovery of gold in the Klondike, which reached the outside world in the summer of 1897, led to nearly every available ship on the coast being diverted to carry men and materials to the Yukon. Realizing this extremely profitable opportunity, CPNC's general manager, Captain John Irving, immediately assigned the *Tees* to the Yukon run and "On sailing nights many Victorians would gather and watch her load her cargo: horses, dogs, and hordes of bewhiskered miners."[6] In 1898, with the *Tees* sailing back and forth to the Yukon, the CPNC purchased the ss *Queen City* and salvaged the ss *Willapa,* which had sunk near Bella Bella. On

The SS *Tees* circa 1910. She began sailing on the west coast run in 1896. She often overlapped with the *Princess Maquinna* until going out of service in 1917. IMAGE C-00588 COURTESY OF THE ROYAL BC MUSEUM.

hearing that the underwriters had declared the SS *Willapa* a total loss, CPNC's manager John Irving sent the *Tees* and a salvage crew north to pump out the hull and tow her to Victoria. Once refurbished, the SS *Willapa* began working the west coast of Vancouver Island route, along with the SS *Queen City,* replacing the *Tees* while she served on the Yukon run.

The passengers on the CPNC ships, particularly those living on Vancouver Island, began voicing dissatisfaction with the haphazard operations of the shipping company. Displeasure grew even louder during the Klondike Gold Rush when the CPNC took many of its best ships from their normal routes to serve on that lucrative run. In 1898 the Victoria Board of Trade wrote to the president of the Canadian Pacific Railway Company, Sir Thomas Shaughnessy, asking him to consider having his company buy out and take over the CPNC. On January 12, 1901, articles in the Victoria and Vancouver newspapers declared that the Canadian Pacific Railway

Company had taken over the CPNC (though its name and livery were in use for another two years). "The announcement will be hailed with great satisfaction on all sides," declared the *Daily Colonist*.[7]

The CPR paid $531,000 to take over the CPNC and its fourteen ships. With the deal complete, the CPR transferred its very capable manager of the Kootenay Lake steamboat operations, Captain James W. Troup, to the coast to act as superintendent. Troup possessed a wealth of experience in shipping. His maternal grandfather, Captain James Turnbull, had been a sailing-ship master, and his father, Captain William H. Troup, had been a well-known riverboat master on the Columbia River. James also became a captain and a riverboat designer, attributes that gave him the necessary pedigree, acumen and experience to run the CPR's new operations.

Born in Portland, Oregon, in 1855, James W. Troup began his career as a deckhand on one of his father's riverboats on the Columbia River at age 17, and by 1878, at age 20, became master of his own steamer, the *Wasp*, and "soon gained fame as a daring and skillful swiftwater pilot."[8] In 1883 Troup came to British Columbia where he took command of the Canadian Pacific Navigation Company's sternwheeler *William Irving*, running on the Fraser River between New Westminster and Yale, and later the sidewheeler *Yosemite*, sailing across the Gulf of Georgia between Victoria and New Westminster. In 1886 he returned to Oregon as superintendent of the Oregon Railway and Navigation Company, but six years later he returned to Nelson in the BC Interior to take charge of the lake and river steamers of the Columbia and Kootenay Navigation Company, which allowed him to not only build but design steamers specifically for that service. In 1897 the Canadian Pacific Railway purchased the Columbia and Kootenay Navigation Company, retaining Troup as its manager. The next year, with the Klondike Gold Rush in full swing, he headed that lucrative operation for his new employer, designing and building four sternwheelers for use on the Yukon and Stikine Rivers, to transport miners and their goods to and from the Yukon goldfields.

By 1901, with the gold rush on the wane, Troup returned to the Kootenay lakes just as the buyout of the Canadian Pacific Navigation Company occurred, and in the same year he moved to Victoria to become the manager of the new CPR coastal service. Once re-branding of the CPNC ships was completed in 1903 the CPR appointed Troup the superintendent of its British Columbia coast service. "For James Troup, the new British Columbia Coast Steamship Service was to be an all-consuming challenge for the remainder of his working life. He put his talents as a ship designer and his persuasive abilities to work immediately and convinced Canadian Pacific's management to build some of the finest coastal liners ever seen on the Pacific Coast."[9]

Troup took over a fleet of fourteen vessels that had come to the CPR from the CPNC, ranging in size from 175 to 1,525 tons, and in age from a few weeks old to forty years. He immediately began planning to upgrade and to add to this fleet. At the time of the takeover, the CPR already ran its elegant, ocean-going *Empress* fleet of stately liners, such as the *Empresses of Canada, Britain* and *Japan*, across both the Atlantic and the Pacific. With these ships foremost in his mind, Troup determined to create a fleet of smaller, but no less opulent, "pocket liners," or *Princess* ships, for the BC coastal service, and to name them after princesses of European royal families. Over the next decade he would design and oversee the building of the first nine of these vessels, which would eventually make up the nineteen-strong fleet of *Princesses*.

> Although not a qualified naval architect, Troup had a vast practical knowledge of ships and shipbuilding. He had had a hand in the building of many river and lake steamers, and he had also helped design the big and luxurious screw steamer *Victorian* intended originally for the Seattle–Victoria run ... and for the years that he was responsible for the *Princesses* he brought into being a long succession of remarkably successful vessels. Each bore very clearly the stamp of his ideas and his experience. Many of the technical details

were worked out by naval architects, but Troup had talents that sometimes enabled him to confound the experts. He had, for example, a singularly sharp eye for the lines of a hull, and once detected a serious error in the calculations of a famous shipyard simply by carefully examining the half-model of the vessel under design.[10]

Troup would dominate every detail of the CPR's west coast fleet's operations over the next twenty-seven years, ensuring that people living on the west coast would have the finest service and ships to serve them. Of all the CPR ships in the fleet, none would prove finer or more beloved than the SS *Princess Maquinna*.

CHAPTER 2

BC BUILT

W HEN CAPTAIN JAMES Troup moved to Victoria in 1901 to become the CPR's West Coast shipping superintendent, he launched a shipbuilding program concentrating on the most profitable CPR routes between the most populous centres: Vancouver to Victoria and Nanaimo, Victoria to Seattle, the Gulf Islands route, the Northern BC and Queen Charlotte run, and the Alaska run. Finally, in 1908, Troup turned his attention to the less lucrative and less populous route along the west coast of Vancouver Island. Although by this point he had participated in designing nine *Princess* ships since becoming superintendent—the *Victoria, Beatrice, Joan, Royal, Charlotte, Adelaide, Mary, Alice* and *Sophia*—Troup knew, even with all his experience, that he faced considerable challenges when he received the go-ahead to build a new *Princess* ship for the west coast run. Seeking help in understanding the conditions his new ship would face, Captain Troup consulted the *Tees* captain, Edward Gillam.

Together Gillam and Troup agreed that the new ship should be double-hulled as a safety measure, given the rocky coast she would travel. They also agreed that the upper deck structure should be kept as low as possible to reduce rolling in the Pacific swells; that all decks, save the top boat deck, should be enclosed by the ship's steel sides; that large observation windows on the promenade deck, characteristic of other *Princess* boats, be eliminated; that the hatches be situated forward, and the cabins, smoking lounge, public rooms and dining room be aft of the hatches (the most comfortable place on a pitching vessel in a storm); and that the aft end be made as sleek as possible to keep the stern from rising in heavy seas, thus preventing the propeller from racing if it lifted clear of the water as the ship plunged into a swell. They also suggested the ship's sides be as perpendicular as possible to enable her to more easily load and unload at west coast wharves in heavy seas and high winds. They planned that the ship would handle four hundred day-passengers, but only provided about fifty staterooms with upper and lower bunks, meaning many passengers would often have to spend nights trying to sleep in the lounge.

By October 1911 shipyards in Britain—and Bullen's shipyard in Esquimalt (the BC Marine Railway Company)—were busy scrutinizing the CPR's seventy-five-page specification document for this new west coast ship, each working hard to earn the contract. For the first time in such a competition, the bids from British shipbuilders came in higher than the local shipyard. J. Mason, assistant to the vice president of the CPR in Winnipeg, wrote to Troup on October 18, 1911: "The President [Sir Thomas Shaughnessy] has tenders now in hand for the west coast steamer, the lowest of which is £44,000 in the Old Country, which is approximately $220,000.00. The cost of getting her out here is about $25,000.00, and then about $5,000.00 for cleaning her up, which would make her cost about $250,000.00 here. Bullen's have agreed to build the same steamer for $250,000.00 here and deliver her to us for that money. We could get a little more for our money in the Old Country in the way of furnishings, but in view of the low figure, I have recommended to the President that we give them the contract."[11] Bullen's readily signed the contract.

Because the steel needed to build the new ship had to be ordered and shipped from Britain, workers at Bullen's yard in Esquimalt could not lay the keel of the new ship until May 1912, after the freighter *Bellerophon* arrived from Britain with the first "… shipment of plates, angles, frames and other components."[12] For the next six months Bullen's workers concentrated on building the hull so that by

The *Princess Maquinna* under construction at Bullen's shipyard in Esquimalt in 1912. IMAGE J-08078 COURTESY OF THE ROYAL BC MUSEUM.

November, when the freighter *Talthybius* arrived in Victoria with the engines, boilers and shafting, they could be quickly inserted into the completed framework. When completed, she was 1,777 tons, 244 ft (71 m) long, 38 ft (13.5 m) wide and with a draft (depth underwater) of 17 ft (7.3 m), making her the largest such ship ever built in British Columbia to that time.

On Christmas Eve 1912, Mrs. Fitzherbert Bullen, wife of the shipyard's owner and the granddaughter of BC's first governor, Sir James Douglas, smashed a bottle of champagne across the bow of the new ship, christening her the SS *Princess Maquinna*, and the ship slipped down the ways into Esquimalt Harbour. "Only those immediately connected with both companies [CPR and BC Marine Railway] saw the fine vessel take to the water, which she did smoothly and gracefully... as soon as the vessel began to move down the ways, Mrs. Fitzherbert Bullen broke the traditional bottle over her prow and christened her after the native princess whose father was Indian Chief at Nootka when that place was visited by early British and Spanish explorers in the 18th Century,"[13] reported the *Daily Colonist* of the launch.

Here again the *Maquinna* stood out from the other *Princess* ships in Troup's fleet, all of which to that date had been named for European princesses. In a letter dated August 14, 1912, Captain Troup wrote to George Bury, vice president and general manager of the CPR in Winnipeg, taking a different direction entirely: "I believe, when you were out here I told you I had a suggestion for a name, and that is 'Princess Maquinna.' I believe, in the past, names have always been submitted to the President for approval. At any rate, I will be glad if you will say if this name is approved. If not, let us have one. My reason for proposing such a name is that once upon a time there was a 'Princess Maquinna' at Nootka Sound, on the west coast of Vancouver Island, the daughter of the old Chief Maquinna, who dominated the Indians at the time Captain Vancouver was there."[14]

On August 28, 1912, Troup received notification that President Shaughnessy had approved the name. On September 6, in a *Daily Colonist* letter to the editor, Captain Frederick Longstaff, who became a noted BC nautical historian, wrote that the credit for suggesting the name actually belonged to Captain John T. Walbran, who commanded CGS *Quadra* from 1891 to 1908, and who in 1909 had published the classic volume *British Columbia Coast Names: Their origin and history*.[15]

Once the SS *Princess Maquinna* settled in the water, the detailed work of fitting out and finishing began. The wooden decks had to be laid and caulked, the cabins built and furnished, the kitchens installed, the dining room completed, the instruments on the bridge put in place, and a host of other tasks finalized before the ship could take her first sea trial and be accepted by the CPR from Bullen's yard. That meticulous work took the better part of five months, and as the ship neared completion a *Colonist* article dated May 6, 1913, could hardly contain itself in praise of the new ship:

> Such splendid progress has been made in the construction of the new Canadian Pacific steamer *Princess Maquinna* during the past few months that the vessel is now rapidly nearing completion at the Esquimalt shipyards of the British Columbia Marine Railway Company, and preliminary arrangements are now underway for her steam trials. The *Princess Maquinna* is undoubtedly the largest and finest vessel that has ever been turned out of a British Columbia shipbuilding plant, and its construction compares favourably with any vessel of her size on the Pacific Coast... The *Maquinna* was designed and built specially for the West Coast of Vancouver Island trade and should prove herself a splendid sea boat in plying the storm-battered coastline. The outstanding feature of the new craft is that all her decks, with the exception of the boat deck, are enclosed by the steel sides of the vessel, and the total absence of housework above the awning deck is a feature that cannot be duplicated by any other vessel plying the Pacific. This handsomely designed coastal craft is considerably longer than the steamer *Princess Royal*, which was the last large steamer to be launched from the BC Marine yards. The *Princess Maquinna*, when finished, will be a marvel of skilled workmanship that could not be excelled in any other shipyard in any part of the world. The building here of such a craft means much to Victoria as a centre of shipbuilding activity, and augurs well for the construction in the immediate future of steamships of much greater dimensions than the one that is about complete at Esquimalt.[16]

The article went on to outline the ship's technical specifications in great detail, before describing the "eight metal, seamless lifeboats, of a size to suit Canadian requirements, 22 feet long," the "complete system of electric lights throughout the vessel," not to mention the firefighting equipment on board, right down to the length of

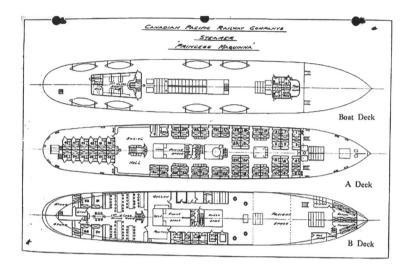

The design of *Maquinna*'s decks, showing the boat deck,
A deck (with the staterooms) and B deck (with the engine room
and freight storage). IMAGE COURTESY OF ROBERT TURNER.

the hoses. As for the speed of this vessel, the *Colonist* breathlessly announced how "the contract calls for a speed of 13½ knots, but it is expected that she will eclipse this during her trials."

The local pride and interest generated by the launch of the *Maquinna* even manifested itself in the name given to a baby girl. Mrs. A.J. Daniels, wife of the shipwright foreman for Bullen's, gave birth to a daughter shortly after the ship's launch. The couple named her Maquinna. Later in life, Maquinna Anderson became an exceptional pianist, well-known throughout British Columbia.[17]

All up and down the west coast of Vancouver Island, local people who had long waited for their new steamer followed every detail of the shipbuilding progress with keen interest. This would be *their* ship, and she was being built especially to serve them. They began making preparations to welcome their new vessel.

As the date of the *Maquinna*'s maiden voyage neared, Captain Troup wrote a letter to Bullen's on July 14, 1913, advising the shipyard that "we expect to bring the 'Princess Maquinna' from Esquimalt to our wharf here [Victoria] tomorrow, Tuesday, and to have her sail on the regular west coast sailing Sunday, July 20th... I propose to go myself as far as Holberg, and would be pleased to have the General Passenger Agent, the General Freight Agent, District Freight Agent or Assistant General Passenger Agent, make the trip also."[18]

In a letter to J. Manson, vice president to CPR president Shaughnessy, Troup wrote on July 15: "After preliminary steam trials 'Princess Maquinna' was taken over by us to-day."[19] The next day the CPR paid the BC Marine Railway Co. the final $30,800 instalment of the $245,000 contract price for building the *Princess Maquinna*.

Four days later, on Sunday, July 20, 1913, Captain Gillam ordered steam from the *Maquinna*'s oil-fired boilers to be injected into the three-cylinder, triple expansion engine. At 11 p.m., as she would do for the next thirty-nine years, the new west coast steamer SS *Princess Maquinna* eased out of the CPR's Belleville Street terminal in Victoria on her maiden voyage up the west coast of Vancouver Island. On board were George Bury, Captain Troup and other dignitaries, as well as members of the general public lucky enough to secure passage at "$24 for the five-day sail, which is less than board and lodging at a decent hotel,"[20] filling up "the greater part of the steamer's accommodation."[21]

A CPR report on the maiden voyage states that when the *Maquinna* eventually reached Bamfield, at the entrance of Alberni Inlet, at 11:05 a.m. the following morning, the entire community was on hand to view the new ship. When docked "a gasoline boat arrived with all flags flying, and a band of music on board. The band was transferred to the 'Princess Maquinna' and at 1:16 p.m. the voyage continued."[22] When the vessel reached Port Alberni at 3:45 p.m., after the 30-mile (50-km) journey down Alberni Inlet, the band began playing on the top deck as a host of launches, small tugs and

floating craft of all description, with bunting and whistles blowing, greeted the *Maquinna*. The industrial whistles of the Canadian
Pacific Lumber Co. mill and the Wiest Logging Company added
to the din. After tying up, the mayor of the city, along with a number of residents of Port Alberni and Old Alberni, assembled in the
ship's dining lounge and addressed Captain Gillam, extending their
congratulations.

Even when the ship arrived at Ucluelet at 4:00 a.m. on July 22,
though "the hour was too early for the citizens to be out ... banners
welcoming the steamer were stretched across the roadway and wharf,
and every evidence of welcome to the new boat was displayed."[23] "At
Clayoquot, Kyuquot and many of the Indian Villages, the Indians
turned out in large numbers to see the new boat, and were very much
interested."[24] "At Kakawis, when the ship stopped at the Christie
Residential School every Indian boy and girl who could get into a
canoe came out alongside. A welcoming salute was fired from an old
Spanish cannon, which is one of the old time relics preserved at this
place. The trip continued without any special incident, on to Nootka,
Kyuquot, Quatsino and Holberg, and great pleasure manifested all
along the line on account of the arrival of the commodious 'Princess
Maquinna' to replace the smaller steamers previously on the route."[25]

Despite the general satisfaction, even when the ship experienced
a heavy westerly blow between Kyuquot and Quatsino, which the
Princess Maquinna handled very well in quite a heavy sea, Captain
Troup noted in his report on the journey:

> One serious matter with the improvement of this service, which
> was brought home to me on this trip, was the inadequacy of the
> wharves. Many of the wharves on the West Coast are literally more
> than half long enough to accommodate a steamer as the *Princess
> Maquinna* and many of them are worm eaten and practically ready
> to fall down; hence I am afraid it will be very difficult to keep a
> boat of her size from doing damage to the wharves, unless they are
> improved. I have done what I could to draw this to the attention of

the Authorities, and hope to have some of them, at least, improved in a short time ... The effective way to bring it about will be to continue the steamer through the summer months and withdraw if the wharves are not improved. This is my present plan, which will no doubt stir up the populace and have the desired effect.[26]

As well as complaining about the west coast wharves, Troup wrote to the BC Marine Railway Co. on July 28, 1913, outlining some defects with the *Maquinna* that were "putting us to considerable expense, in fact, serious expense, and for which we must hold you responsible."[27] The baffle plate in the condenser had come loose; the reverse gear cylinder proved defective; the winch drum on the starboard side was bent; the steering gear did not work well and did not allow the ship to come over hard to starboard; the boiler stays were inserted too rigidly, causing the rivets to leak; and the soil pipes in the water closet on the main deck were found to be blocked.

In August 1913, despite the rousing welcome and the high hopes of west coast residents for their future transport, Captain Troup removed the *Maquinna* from the west coast route to make a special run to Alaska, replacing her with the *Tees*. The *Maquinna* took seventy delegates north to Skagway to attend the International Geological Congress, and while on that voyage she suffered the first of many mishaps she would experience in her lifetime, when she struck an uncharted rock in Yakutat Bay, Alaska. On her return to Victoria, Troup ordered the *Maquinna* hauled up the ways of the BC Marine yards at Esquimalt to replace twenty dented plates and attend to the list of other repairs, at a cost of $12,000. She returned to her west coast Vancouver Island route for the fall of 1913, but in January 1914 Troup again placed her back on the Alaska run, where she gained much favour for her seaworthiness and fine accommodations. People living on the west coast were most chagrined at having had the SS *Tees*, once again, foisted on them.

Few ever described the *Tees* as elegant: "she was sturdy, reliable, and by all accounts impressively ugly,"[28] writes Margaret Horsfield

Occasionally, the *Princess Maquinna* needed to go into dry
dock for repairs. Here she is in 1916, on the ways at the Wallace
Shipyard in Victoria, undergoing minor repairs to her hull.

IMAGE VPL 20028 COURTESY OF THE VANCOUVER PUBLIC LIBRARY.

in *Voices from the Sound*. Captain Adam Smith, who sailed her from
Britain to Victoria, stated that a better sea boat was never built, and
that "She rides the water like a duck."[29]

Not all agreed. "It was popularly conceded that the wallowing old
tub never sheared the water, she pushed it ahead of her," wrote Tofino's Mike Hamilton in his memoirs. "Boy, that blinking old tub could
roll and take a nose dive at the same time, so much so that hardened
sailors got seasick on her..." and, as for her cabins, they were "more
like the accommodation that would be provided for the Slobovians
of L'il Abner fame... with a 'chamber' pot provided, and a ewer and
basin; a narrow hard bunk and I can't remember if we had electric
light."[30] (She did.) But lighting did nothing to improve Nan Beere's
memories of the ship. Youngest daughter of Harlan Brewster, the
Clayoquot Cannery owner and future premier of the province, Nan

recalled that the *Tees* became known as the "Holy Roller," legendary for the seasickness she caused as she pitched and rolled her way up the coast. "I was sick thirteen times on one voyage on the *Tees*," she recalls. "Into a white hat, I remember."[31] On February 26, 1914, the *Daily Colonist* reported:

> In replying to criticisms levelled against the company in connection with the withdrawal of *Princess Maquinna* from West Coast Vancouver Island (WCVI) route, Capt Troup remarked that the Maquinna was an expensive boat to operate on the WCVI during the winter months, when the freight business was at its lowest ebb. He stated that when the company built the *Maquinna* it was looking to the future with the object of building up a big tourist trade between Victoria and WCVI, and he emphasized the point that during the winter months when the tourist travel was nil, such a boat as the *Maquinna* was operating at a loss. "As a matter of fact," said Capt Troup, "The *Maquinna* last December failed to do anything like the business *Tees* brought in during the same period of the previous year." The result was that the losses to the company were exceptionally heavy in operating the *Maquinna* during November and December. During the spring and summer months the CPR expected to build up a big trade with the WCVI, when the *Maquinna*, with her superior passenger accommodation, will be a paying proposition.[32]

True to his word, in early April 1914 Troup put the *Maquinna* back on the west coast run, where her return "will be hailed with joy by the inhabitants of that route, who resented the temporary withdrawal of the steamer from the service."[33]

Soon after Troup reinstated the *Maquinna*, Captain Longstaff took the opportunity to travel on her up the west coast. He praised the seaworthy qualities of the ship and presciently suggested that the *Princess Maquinna* "will speedily become one of the most popular excursions for visitors to the Island. The beautiful scenery, the

The *Princess Maquinna* tied up to the dock at Tofino.
IMAGE PN 13047 COURTESY OF THE ALBERNI VALLEY MUSEUM.

constant variety of the Coast and its primitive Indian settlements whence the natives come out in their canoes to handle their own freight, all combine to make it an experience altogether out of the common and especially fascinating to those who are paying a visit to the Island for the first time."[34] She would sail from Victoria on the 1st, 10th and 20th of each month to Holberg in Quatsino Sound, but on the trip of the 10th she would omit some intermediate stops, making for a faster journey than on the 1st and 20th trips. So popular would she become that, despite temporary departures, the *Maquinna* would run up and down the west coast almost without interruption for the next thirty-nine years.

CHAPTER 3

FIRST STOP

ETURNING TO our imagined summer cruise in 1924, once the ship sails past the entrance to Esquimalt Harbour, she continues offshore of the Esquimalt Lagoon and Royal Roads. If it was daytime instead of 11:30 in the evening, passengers could have glimpsed the palatial, forty-room Hatley Castle, stately home of coal baron and former BC premier and lieutenant governor James Dunsmuir. Although Dunsmuir died in 1920, four years later his widow still lives there. In 1940 the Department of National Defence would purchase the property, turning it into the Royal Roads Military College, and later the Department of National Defence leased the land for use by Royal Roads University.

About 8 nautical miles (15 km) further on, after the ship has steamed past Metchosin's Albert Head Lighthouse, the Race Rocks Lighthouse appears, warning of the dangerous rocks and the even more dangerous tidal currents "racing" around them. Keeping that light well to starboard (while remaining in Canadian waters, as the border with the United States lies in mid-channel), the *Maquinna* picks up even more speed, heading into the Strait of Juan de Fuca. Turning northwestward into the strait, which measures between 10 and 15 nautical miles wide (18 to 27 km), the ship and her passengers begin to feel the first effects of the Pacific swells.

At this stage of the journey, first-class passengers are settling into their bunks under crisp, clean sheets and eiderdowns. Second-class passengers in their four-berth cabins are getting to know their fellow cabin mates as they choose their upper or lower bunks. In the lounge, those who have chosen the second-class option but not paid for a berth in a four-bunk cabin stake their claim on the couchettes and nestle in for a fitful sleep. Outside on the deck, First Nations people settle down among their baggage, including blankets, mats, pots, pans and other cooking utensils, and try, as CP inspector H.W. Brodie described in his 1918 report, "to make themselves as comfortable as possible, and, Indian fashion, taking everything as it comes."[35]

On the bridge, Captain Gillam keeps a watchful eye as the *Maquinna* steams at a comfortable 10½ knots past the entrance to Sooke Harbour. If Gillam requires more speed, he can order his engineer to take the ship up to its maximum speed of 13½ knots, but that would only hurt the Canadian Pacific's bottom line, using too much oil to fire the ship's boilers. Troup, back in his office in Victoria, constantly reminds his captains of the need to be economical, especially on this west coast run, rated as one of CP's least profitable routes.

Captain Gillam is a favourite of all who sail on the *Maquinna*, from crew to passengers. "In a photograph of unknown date, he appears as a robust-looking man with a military bearing, a trim mustache and a kindly expression," writes Tony Guppy in his book *The Tofino Kid*:

> He had the far-seeing gaze of a mariner and obviously belonged to that breed of seafarers who were absolutely dedicated to their work. It was well known that every trip he made, no matter how routine, was carefully planned. Every turn of the tide, every eventuality, fog or storm, the time of arrival at every port, would have been judiciously overseen and arranged for the comfort and safety of his passengers. In fact, if necessary, schedules were abandoned in the interests of passenger safety and well-being and stops were missed out altogether if, for example, a passenger was taken sick and needed medical attention. Captain Gillam would stay on the

Captain Gillam with an unidentified woman and child, date unknown.
IMAGE PN 04450 COURTESY OF THE ALBERNI VALLEY MUSEUM.

bridge many hours without sleep when conditions were bad, and this would be the usual, rather than the unusual. In the winter and fall months, dense fogs would blow in to blanket the coast, and sudden gale force winds would kick up mighty seas.[36]

On this night calm summer weather prevails, making for smooth sailing. Five hours after departure, at just after 4 a.m., and 57 nautical miles (105 km) out from Victoria, the *Maquinna* reaches her first stop at Port Renfrew, named after Lord Renfrew who planned on settling Scottish crofters in the area in the 1880s. Situated at the head of San Juan Inlet, and at the mouth of the San Juan and Jordan Rivers, the community originally bore the name Port San Juan, so dubbed by Spanish navigator Manuel Quimper in 1790. This small fishing and logging port, with a population of about one hundred, most employed by the Defiance Packing Company cannery, changed its name to Port Renfrew in 1895, because mail bound for another San Juan in the American San Juan Islands often showed up here by mistake.

Open to the unbroken power of the Pacific, the long pier at Port Renfrew makes for difficult docking, and in stormy weather the *Maquinna*'s deck crew needs to use six hawsers, or docking lines, to hold her in place, but in calm weather, three holds will do. If heavy swells are running the deck crew is kept busy constantly tending the hawsers and in such weather the loading doors remain closed and all cargo for Port Renfrew must be off-loaded using the ship's derricks. As soon as the winches and derricks begin clattering and banging, the passengers in their cabins awake with a start and find themselves lying wide awake because of the "unholy row."[37]

Between 1901 and 1907, before the *Maquinna* serviced Port Renfrew, a unique and unlikely group of students and instructors from the American Midwest arrived here on the ss *Tees* and the ss *Queen City,* the *Maquinna*'s predecessors. In those six summers, the landlocked Midwesterners, mainly from Minnesota, Ohio and Nebraska, travelled first by rail across the United States to Seattle and then by ship to Victoria before heading up the west coast, to study the sea life and geology of an extraordinary area now known as Botanical Beach, 2.5 miles (4 km) southwest of Port Renfrew. Once disembarked, the groups of thirty or so students, including many young women, hiked through the forest along an "appallingly rough, muddy"[38] trail for four hours, packing all their belongings as well as food and supplies to the site they called the Minnesota Seaside Station. There, the students immersed themselves in studying the rich sea life that abounds in the unusually deep tidal pools, hewn out of the sandstone over millennia by the pounding waves.

The dream of biologist Dr. Josephine Tilden, this seaside station provided the students with a rare opportunity to do Pacific Coast field-study work. The students thrived here, even though many had never seen the sea before. "The challenges of fieldwork at the seaside station required the women to plunge into tidal pools, teeter along slippery logs in the dark, slog over muddy trails carrying heavy luggage—some even donned men's overalls, amid gales of laughter, for the long hikes. They had never been so free, or so far from home, and they loved it."[39]

Despite the success of the program and the enthusiasm of the two hundred or so students who came to the Minnesota Seaside Station during the six years it operated, and although Josephine Tilden was using her own funds to support it, the program ended in 1907 because the regents of the University of Minnesota announced that the university "could not own and operate buildings and grounds within the confines of a foreign country,"[40] ending one of the many curious and improbable ventures that have flourished and died on the west coast.

Back at the Port Renfrew dock, the clatter of the *Princess Maquinna*'s winches, and the general racket created by the off-loading and loading of cargo, makes sleep impossible for most passengers. Soon, however, with the ship stopped, a new sound echoes along the passageways outside their cabin doors, as a steward beats out a tune on his xylophone-like chimes shouting out: "First call to breakfast, first call to breakfast!" With that, passengers make their way along the passageways to the dining saloon at the aft end of the main deck to partake of the first of six meals the galley serves each day—two sittings each of breakfast, lunch and dinner. The guests enter the dining room, capable of seating ninety people, to a space fitted with large portholes arranged so that, as far as practical, each table sits opposite a porthole, allowing plentiful natural light to shine into the saloon. Mahogany panelling covers the walls, set with cornices and plaster; the deck is made of Oregon pine, the ceilings panelled with cedar and painted white. The tables lie covered by white damask tablecloths, with silver place settings and gleaming chinaware,

The dining room on the *Princess Norah*, shown here, was
comparable to the *Princess Maquinna*'s, with both ships,
like all CPR vessels, providing exceptional food and service.
IMAGE D-02715 COURTESY OF THE ROYAL BC MUSEUM.

including teapots, cream jugs and sugar bowls, all embossed with
the insignia of the Canadian Pacific. White-jacketed waiters stand
by the tables, an immaculate tea towel folded over their left arms.

Take a seat, and start breakfast with a bowl of stewed prunes—
familiarly known as "CPR strawberries" because of their ubiquitous
presence on the menus of all CP ships and trains—"as if the railroad
company had in mind before anything else the regularity and good
digestive health of its passengers."[41] Follow these with a hearty plate
of porridge laden with brown sugar and real cream, and afterwards
tuck into a plate of fried bacon, eggs and toast, washed down with
tea or coffee. Thus fortified, passengers face a leisurely morning's

travel, awaiting the steward's next gong to bring them back to the dining room to partake of luncheon.

An hour and twenty-five minutes after arriving, with Port Renfrew's cargo off-loaded and some new passengers welcomed aboard, the *Maquinna* backs away from the dock and heads northward. In calm summer weather, this next leg of the route makes for sedate and pleasant sailing, but in winter, when storms rage, these waters have proven to be some of the most dangerous and perilous on the west coast of the Americas, claiming hundreds of lives and scores of ships.

CHAPTER 4

THE TRAIL

I N THE TWENTY-FIRST century, thousands of hikers lace up their boots every summer and set forth on the rugged hike along what is now known as the West Coast Trail. For this 47-mile (75-km) hike, which usually takes between five and seven days to complete, they load their backpacks with a sleeping bag, tent, food, wet gear and changes of clothes. Stretching from Port Renfrew to Bamfield on Vancouver Island's west coast, the trail has grown so popular that hikers must reserve months in advance, and pay a hefty fee, to be allowed to embark on what many call "the trip of a lifetime." The trek can be hazardous, some hikers at times suffering injuries and exhaustion, but such setbacks are minor in comparison with the death and disasters that occurred along this stretch of coast a century or more ago.

Throughout the nineteenth century, sailing ships lay at the mercy of strong southeast gales and powerful currents that drove many of them onto the rocks and beaches of Vancouver Island's exposed west coast, in particular between Port Renfrew and Bamfield. This section of the coast became known as "the Graveyard of the Pacific." In the forty years prior to 1906, 56 vessels foundered and 711 people lost their lives[42] on this hazardous stretch. Because of this loss of life, the Canadian Federal Government provided funds to build the Dominion Life Saving Trail, or Shipwrecked Mariner's Trail, with the aim of aiding survivors of ships wrecked along that portion of the west coast.

Sailing ships heading into Victoria and Puget Sound from the Pacific Ocean often hove to at the entrance to the Strait of Juan de Fuca, where it is 12 nautical miles (22 km) wide, waiting for contract-seeking steam-driven tugs to come out and tow them into safer waters. However, with no radio communication, storms or fog often prevented those tugs from finding the waiting windjammers, and the tugs and ships often did not make contact. "Standing out to sea certainly offered no assurance of safety," writes Ted Rogers in his *Shipwrecks of British Columbia.* "So long as visibility was fair and the guiding beacon of Cape Flattery could be seen, the old-time skipper had a winning chance. But when the weather thickened, it was inevitable that his ship would ride on the offshore current sweeping the coast of Washington and the shores of Vancouver Island. At times the current, aided by a strong southeaster, would carry a vessel a considerable distance before danger was recognized."[43] Strong and prolonged southeastern gales drove sailing ships up and onto the rocks and the shores of southwestern Vancouver Island, and sometimes took them well up the coast, occasionally as far as the Gulf of Alaska.

With no reliable weather forecasts to warn of impending danger, ships fully laden with lumber, ore or other products also headed out of the Strait of Juan de Fuca, and even in summer they could encounter storms and thick fog. "If a bearing was not obtained from some recognizable landmark and the ship was out of horn range," Rogers writes, referring to Cape Flattery's foghorn, "the skipper knew he could be in for trouble. Sometimes the fog would lift for a spell to reveal a point of land. If 'the old man' was able to identify his landfall, he was reasonably safe continuing on course; if he was mistaken—and such was the case all too often—his ship would end up on the treacherous rocks with all hands lost ... Each year, the foaming reefs of Vancouver Island's east and west coast would be strewn with the wreckage of ill-fated ships which had become trapped near the shore in storm or fog."[44]

In response to this danger, the Federal Government's Department of Marine and Fisheries built a number of lighthouses—Cape

Beale in 1873 and Carmanah Point in 1890—and supplied some communities, including Bamfield and Tofino, with lifeboats. However, it took one of the worst maritime disasters in BC history to instigate the building of the Dominion Life Saving Trail, later known as the West Coast Trail. In 1906, while seeking the entrance to the Strait of Juan de Fuca, the passenger ship SS *Valencia* ran aground off Pachena Point near the southern entrance to Barkley Sound. The ship was over 27 nautical miles (50 km) off course on its run from San Francisco to Seattle and Victoria. One hundred and thirty-six people lost their lives when the ship steamed, at 11 knots, up onto the rocks.[45] The disaster prompted the Canadian government to launch a Commission of Inquiry, which recommended the construction of a Dominion Life Saving Trail along the edge of the coast that would allow shipwrecked passengers and crew to make their way on foot north (to Bamfield) or south (to Port Renfrew) to get help.

In June 1907, using the $30,000, or $1,000 per mile, allocated by the Federal Government to begin the project, a crew of "... 30 or 40 workmen,"[46] under the direction of foreman J. McDonald, began building the trail, starting at the north end near Bamfield. Using hand tools and a few horses and cutting whatever lumber they required from the abundance of nearby trees, by the end of October they had completed 22 miles (35.4 km) of trail, or nearly half the distance required.

The workmen followed the route of an already existing telegraph line that, between 1889 and 1891, had been strung from tree to tree along trails used for centuries by the First Nations people of the area. The trail had a full view of the ocean for most of its route, even using foreshore beaches. At the northern end, from Bamfield to Pachena Point, the trail proved easy to build, allowing it to be 12 ft (3.5 m) wide, but for the rest of its more rugged journey the trail is only 4 ft (1.2 m) wide. The harsh terrain required the trail builders to construct 130 bridges and 70 ladders, and when they encountered four very deep river gorges, they fashioned aerial trolleys with boatswain's chairs hanging from them. People using the trail pulled themselves

Hikers in recent times make their way up one of the many staircases on the West Coast Trail. IMAGE COURTESY OF JASON HUMMEL.

over the gorges using a continuous loop of wire (not unlike a clothes-line) while sitting in the boatswain's chairs. Every 5 miles (8 km) or so along the trail, the workers constructed small cabins, equipping them with blankets and rations as well as directions and maps of the trail. Each cabin also contained a telegraph key connected to the nearby telegraph wire, with instruction in several languages on its use. Two Lyle rocket guns were stationed at the Bamfield Creek and Clo-oose cabins. These enabled local inhabitants to aid in nearby rescues by bringing a horse to carry the heavy guns down to the shoreline, where they used them to fire a rocket with lifelines attached to a distressed ship so that survivors might perhaps be able to reach shore.

Work continued on the trail for four years. When finally completed in 1911 the Department of Marine and Fisheries arranged for coast guards to patrol the trail daily to ensure the telegraph line remained intact and to look out for vessels in distress. Once finished, the trail needed constant repairs, especially to fix damage done by winter storms. This work was carried out by men like John Logan, who lived at Clo-oose from 1894 until his death in 1938. Logan became legendary for his dedicated work as a telegraph lineman and as a trail custodian, and for saving many shipwreck survivors over the years.

The Dominion Life Saving Trail, as it was known, had been fully operational for two years before the *Princess Maquinna* began plying her way up and down the west coast. Mercifully, neither she nor her passengers would ever make use of it, nor could they glimpse any sign of it from the ship's position offshore as we follow her course in 1924. But the trail was there for them and for all who sailed or steamed up the west coast, serving as a constant reminder of the dangers of the waters on which they travelled.

CHAPTER 5

BOAT LANDINGS

STEAMING NORTHWARD from Port Renfrew, after an hour and a half the *Maquinna* reaches the first of the three most tricky and perilous stops on the vessel's entire journey. Carmanah Lighthouse, Clo-oose and Nitinat all require boat landings, meaning there is no dock to tie up to and passengers and goods have to be off-loaded into rowboats or canoes in open water while the ship heaves to—or holds its position—against the incoming waves. Before this can occur, Captain Gillam carefully assesses the weather, the tide, the Pacific swells and the overall conditions in order to decide whether to stop at each of these places or whether to carry on and hopefully make a stop on the *Maquinna*'s returning southbound journey instead. Should the conditions prove fine, the ship heaves to as close as possible to shore, turns her bow out to sea to meet the oncoming swells and drops anchor, all the while keeping her engines ticking over with enough power to hold her in position. On one occasion at Clo-oose the *Maquinna* bumped her keel on the sandy seabed, whereupon Captain Gillam did not even wait to haul anchor, but let it go, chain and all, and headed out to sea.

At the Carmanah Lighthouse, built in 1890 and run by six people, small rowboats make their way out from Carmanah Point, on which the lighthouse sits, to the freight doors at the side of the *Maquinna*. There, the goods for the light station are precariously off-loaded into the bobbing boats and rowed to the bottom of the headland where they are loaded onto a gasoline-powered trolley atop a tramway to be taken up to the lighthouse.

Prior to the *Maquinna*'s arrival on the west coast, when the SS *Tees* served this route, W.P. Daykin held the position as Carmanah lightkeeper from 1891 to 1912. His daily log contains many stories of rowboats being swamped or overturned, ruining precious supplies. He "expressed frustration when foodstuffs—especially his supply of liquor—was carried back and forth several times, because of bad weather, before it could be landed. Since there was no refrigeration on the small steamer, his meat proved unfit for human consumption by the time it eventually landed—and the lightkeeper bore the financial loss as well as the loss of his food."[47] On one occasion, with the weather too stormy for the supply steamer to call for a full month, Daykin finally received his forty pounds of bacon, to find it so ripe and "ALIVE" he sent it back on board. So frustrated did Daykin become with such misadventures and the loneliness of Carmanah, that he reputedly was consuming a bottle of Scotch a day for "medicinal purposes." Despite his drinking, however, he continued conscientiously doing his job until transferred to Macaulay Point Lighthouse at the entrance to Victoria Harbour in 1912.

Half an hour and 4 nautical miles (7.5 km) north of the Carmanah Lighthouse, the *Maquinna* heaves to off Clo-oose, which means "safe landing" in the language of the local Ditidaht people. It is anything but a "safe landing" site for a sizeable steamer. Clo-oose lies exposed to the force of wind and waves coming across the vastness of the Pacific Ocean, making it an impossible place to build a dock. It is the kind of place more beloved by surfers than by ships trying to disembark people and goods onto an open shoreline. Despite the difficulty of access, Clo-oose possesses a long and interesting story of settlement, ranking it among the most improbable pioneering stories in a province noted for such ventures.

An economic boom before World War I saw a rush of buyers purchasing raw land all over the province of British Columbia. Local newspapers were crammed full of advertisements offering lots for

Rowboats await their turn to load passengers and goods
at the side of the *Princess Maquinna* off Clo-oose.

Many Clo-oose settlers came from Britain having bought plots
of land "sight unseen" before arriving. Here patriotic settlers
pose on the beach flanked by Union Jacks. IMAGE AEGL0001002A
COURTESY OF THE BAMFIELD HISTORICAL SOCIETY.

sale, sometimes in the most unlikely locations. From the late 1890s
immigrants had arrived in Canada from overseas in the thousands,
in a land-rush bonanza initially fuelled by Prime Minister Wilfrid
Laurier's federal government offering 160 acres of free prairie land
to lure people to come and settle that vast and harsh environment.
Laurier's plan succeeded in attracting more than 1.5 million settlers
to put down roots on the prairies between 1896 and 1911. With
robust economic times seeming to last forever, people looked for
similar opportunities to buy cheap land in other parts of Canada.
Many arrived having little idea of what they would face; this was
certainly so on the west coast of Vancouver Island, perhaps the most
dramatic example being at Clo-oose.

Into this milieu stepped a number of unscrupulous real estate
developers associated with the Victoria firm of Monk, Monteith
and Co. Ltd., "one of the largest and most influential real estate

Fanciful artist's renderings in the West Coast Development Company's brochure hoped to entice prospective buyers to purchase land at Clo-oose. The West Coast Development Company proposed building a three-hundred-room hotel like this at Clo-oose. It was never built.

IMAGES FROM 93-7330 EARL MARSH ACCESSION BOX 3,

COURTESY OF THE ROYAL BC MUSEUM.

and insurance firms in Victoria."[48] A group of these men incorporated the West Coast Development Company in 1912 with the aim of developing a seaside resort community at Clo-oose, boasting that it would become "Canada's Greatest Pleasure Resort." The company printed attractive, colourful thirty-page brochures complete with stylized graphics and photographs to lure prospective buyers, distributing their propaganda far and wide. Lavish proposals for development promised a splendid three-hundred-room hotel—not unlike the CPR hotels at Lake Louise and Banff Springs—featuring tennis courts, croquet and bowling greens, and a golf course, as well as offering to stage light operas and vaudeville acts during the summer months. In addition it touted a sandy beach 9 miles (14.5 km) long—a considerable exaggeration—from which the driftwood would be removed, plus medicinal springs, incomparable salmon and trout fishing, and hunting without parallel. Amazingly, they also promised that there were absolutely no flies or mosquitoes. As an added incentive, the promoters offered a $10,000 cash prize and a $1,000 bungalow to the buyer who came up with a name for the resort.

Once incorporated, the company purchased lots 56, 57 and 70 in the Renfrew Land District, which it subdivided into 5,000 lots of 33 by 66 ft (10 by 20 m)—which was even smaller than the average city lot—and put them up for sale at $150 to $200 per lot. Road allowances were cleared and trails were made to provide temporary access to the lots until such time as roads could be completed. The old SS *Tees* would initially provide transportation from Victoria, but the brochure promised she "... would shortly be succeeded by a magnificent new steamer called the *Princess Maquinna*."[49] The developers even promised a Canadian National Railway spur line— backed by the provincial government—to connect the development to Lake Cowichan in the middle of the island. It would never be built. They even petitioned the BC government to change the name of Clooose to Clovelly. That also never happened.

An artist's sketch, drawn for the promoters, whose imaginations had run wild, depicted long wharves flanked by cargo ships, wide streets, fine buildings and a street railway fronting a magnificent white beach lapped by the sparkling blue waters of the Pacific Ocean.

Soon some two hundred settlers arrived and began establishing themselves temporarily in tents along the beach, while building more permanent log cabins for themselves and their families. Many of these settlers came from Britain, having fallen under the spell of the advertising campaign. They began by felling the enormous trees nearby and hauling them to the site. Few of these settlers had ever faced such a harsh or forbidding environment before, and were entirely out of their element. Angela Newitt, who came from England to Clo-oose as a three-year-old wrote: "Poor Daddy, I don't know what he thought he was going to do in Canada. He had left a nice cushy job with Prudential Life in London, where his hobby was the Royal Horticulture Society and growing prize roses for the show. His passport to Canada described him as a 'Gentleman Farmer'!"[50]

Some who arrived didn't stay long enough to fight it out with the elements. "One family from Alberta, who came without any preliminary inspection direct to Clo-oose—sold up everything and saw all their goods going ashore by dugout from the *Maquinna*. The story has it that they asked for the city hall—they left on the return voyage abandoning most of their possessions."[51]

The developers did build one edifice, the Bungalow Inn, where some of the newly arrived settlers stayed until they found their properties. "The Inn was a large dining room with a huge stone fireplace. There were no bedrooms. Most guests lived outside in tents, some of the larger ones with 'camp-keeping' facilities, and were served meals in the Inn. Those living inside the building lived in sections partitioned off by blankets. As one old-timer said, 'You knew where you lived by the colour of the blankets'!"[52]

Some of the settlers took up farming, perhaps convinced by the promotional brochures that glowingly described "the Island's rain forests as the last frontier of virgin soil . . . [where one] could grow potatoes the size of footballs, and corn as tall as trees . . ."[53]

The settlers fought off cougars and packs of feral dogs that attacked their livestock, as well as incessant rain and winds, occasionally finding comfort in parties, dances and social gatherings. One of the odder newcomers "used to dress in formal wear for dinner and entertain his guests on a player piano. In order to accommodate them he built bleachers at one end of his large dining-room."[54]

"Very little news of the outside world got through to us," writes Newitt. "The boat rarely called in winter, and Mother said that we didn't know there was a war on [World War I began in August 1914]

A family of settlers in their tent on the beach at Clo-oose, 1919.
IMAGE COURTESY OF THE BAMFIELD HISTORICAL SOCIETY.

'til the first boat arrived in the spring of 1915. As soon as this news arrived, most men . . . left to join up, my father amongst them."[55] Of the thirty-one men of Clo-oose who went overseas to fight in this devastating war, eleven died, including Newitt's father. Clo-oose gained the distinction of sending more men per capita to World War I than any other place in Canada.[56] Although late in joining the rush to go overseas, the men from Clo-oose joined hundreds of others from other small communities up and down the west coast of Vancouver Island who boarded the *Princess Maquinna* on the first leg of their journey to the battlefields of France and Belgium.

With the loss of so many men, the women of Clo-oose found it increasingly difficult to maintain themselves and their children in such an isolated location with no amenities whatever, ceaseless hard work, increasing loneliness and with no sign of the promised development coming to fruition. They began leaving for Victoria. When the soldiers returned in 1918 and 1919, those who made their way back to Clo-oose found hard economic times and very little work, even though following the war the Lummi Bay Cannery opened at the nearby mouth of Nitinat Lake, and the Nitinat Logging Company also provided some employment for a time. But the cannery closed in 1921, and yet more settlers gave up and left. Nevertheless some people did hang on, relying on the *Princess Maquinna* as their connection to the outside world, and as long as people remained, the boat landings continued, requiring the skills of the Ditidaht paddlers in their hand-hewn dugout canoes to transfer passengers and their goods to and from the shore.

The First Nations paddlers brought their canoes alongside the *Maquinna*'s open cargo doors at the side of the ship where a crewman, harnessed to the hull, readied loads of goods, preparing to lower them.

The dugouts manoeuvred alongside the rolling vessel and, at just that instant when the canoe was on top of a swell, the sling load was dropped into the canoe while it was fended off from the ship's side. Passengers were unloaded the same way, females as well as males.

Landing supplies at Clo-oose in the 1920s with the *Princess Maquinna* standing to in the background. IMAGE PN 04315 COURTESY OF THE ALBERNI VALLEY MUSEUM.

They stood poised at the open freight door of the ship, ready to jump at the critical moment. If they jumped too soon they met the canoe as it surged upward on the swell and anything might happen; if they jumped too late, they had ten or twelve feet to fall to the bottom of the canoe as it sank in a trough.[57]

Sometimes, usually in calm weather, disembarking passengers could climb down a rope ladder to the canoes. Miss Hardwick, who arrived in Clo-oose in 1906, when her father came as a timber cruiser, relates that "one had to very carefully time their jump from the swinging rope ladder to the swaying canoe, it was, to say the least, a precarious mode of disembarkation and, more than once, ill-fated. Once [...] a missionary's wife had had to swim ashore unaided when she missed her 'step' into a waiting canoe."[58]

"Tourists marvelled at the way such frail craft were manipulated," writes George Nicholson in *Vancouver Island's West Coast*:

Usually, the canoes were handled by 'one old Indian with a short paddle,' as a younger native squatted in the stern to catch the freight as it was tossed from the ship. Occasionally a passenger had to be taken ashore the same way and if it happened to be a woman, camera-armed tourists got a greater thrill. Watching the heavily-laden canoes go ashore was just as exciting, especially as they neared the beach where, regardless of how smooth the sea appeared to be, the swells always broke. More so when it was really rough and a ducking for someone and wet freight usually resulted.[59]

"Landing conditions were often not ideal," writes R.E. Wells in *There's a Landing Today*:

The canoes would sometimes put off in rough seas, the residents determined to land whatever the ship had for them. A canoe could get caught under the heavy guard rail of the ship and before the paddlers could fend off, it would be flipped over with men and contents. Sometimes the flour, which had been ordered from town weeks before, would at the last moment get soaked. There was a time when a baby, being so well wrapped against the elements, was passed down from the mother and, in the hurry of the moment and with the rising and falling swell, was placed face down in the canoe. With the amount of water that the canoe had shipped, the poor little one was almost overcome.[60]

Drama over, the *Maquinna* ups anchor and heads out to sea, rounding Carmanah Point and steaming north once again. She will make other boat landings on her way up and down the west coast, at Kakawis, Refuge Cove and Hesquiaht, but none of these hold the peril, precision and sheer excitement of the two stops at Carmanah and Clo-oose.

CHAPTER 6

SEEING THE SIGHTS

B Y MID- TO LATE morning, depending on the quantity of goods and the number of passengers landed and loaded at Clo-oose, Captain Gillam charts a course northward, a safe distance offshore. With any luck, passengers can, for a brief period—should the weather be sunny and the seas calm—enjoy extraordinary views of the rugged shoreline. Experienced coastal travellers know better, though, than to count on such idyllic conditions.

With the *Maquinna* barely underway, about 1.6 nautical miles (3 km) north of Clo-oose, passengers strain to pick out the entrance to the channel leading into Nitinat Lake. This channel, which extends that same length, bisects the West Coast Trail and connects the partially saltwater Nitinat Lake to the Pacific Ocean by way of a constricted tidal estuary measuring barely 100 ft (30 m) across at its narrowest point. Locally known as "the Gap," currents surge through this opening at an alarming 8 knots, and the passage has capsized or sunk "more boats, with considerable loss of life, than at any other passage of its kind on the British Columbia Coast," according to George Nicholson in *Vancouver Island's West Coast*.[61] To make navigating the Gap even more dangerous, a shallow sandbar lurks only a few metres below the surface on the outer side of the entrance. And in a final twist of danger, a reef known as Sawtooth Rock lies just under the breaking surf only 250 ft (75 m) from the sandbar.

Local lore dictates that to travel safely through the Gap any boats entering Nitinat Lake from the sea—and none larger than a fishboat or a medium-sized tugboat can even attempt it—must keep to the right of the channel when attempting the passage in the six minutes during slack tide. They should then let the current carry the vessel along rather than employ much engine power. Long-time west-coaster Ernest Logan tells of his experience going through the Gap:

> I had some good rides over the Nitinat bar, but I enjoyed them all, lots of fun. I got turned over there once in my fish-boat. That was the first time I'd seen a boat up-end! She didn't roll over, she up-ended! She climbed the breaker and then the curl threw her right over. The hardest thing I ever tried to ride was the bottom of that boat, upside down, slippery with copper paint, and nothing to hold on to![62]

The Lummi Bay Cannery lies just inside Nitinat Lake, and knowledgeable fishboat skippers delivering fish to the plant generally make the passage with little incident. Others, not possessing such a wealth of local knowledge, often come to grief. However, even highly experienced captains could misjudge these waters, sometimes with tragic consequences. Back in November 1918 a local fish-packer, the *Renfrew*, left the cannery carrying twenty-six jubilant cannery workers, all happy to be leaving after an isolated summer's work. A large breaker struck the boat halfway through the Gap. The wave smashed a skylight causing water to stall the engine. An anchor thrown overboard failed to stop the boat going broadside and capsizing. Those below decks failed to get out, drowning thirteen of them. The Ditidaht people at Whyac—the village just inside the entrance—helped save the rest of those onboard.

The *Maquinna* only makes infrequent calls to service the needs of the cannery and the Ditidaht. On such occasions, as at Clo-oose, the experienced Indigenous paddlers come out in their canoes through the Gap to unload and load passengers and goods from the *Maquinna*'s cargo door.

Weather permitting, a few miles farther north Captain Gillam eases the *Maquinna* closer to shore, allowing passengers to more easily view the coast and to use their KODAK Brownie box cameras to take photographs. Sea caves and blowholes, caused by wave action eroding the roof of a cave, are visible; also seastacks, promontories and miles-long sandy beaches. Passengers can marvel at large colonies of sea lions lounging on the rocks, belching and barking. Eagles circle overhead on constant lookout for prey. Orcas might even appear, known at that time as black fish or killer whales.

Some geological features can be heard, as well as seen. Near the Nitinat Gap, one particularly large blowhole, of which there are many, lets off a mighty roar and a whistling sound at high tide that passengers may hear as the water shoots up and out of the opening, wooshing high into the air. Passing skippers often "mistook the noise for a foghorn, looked in vain for a lighthouse when the fog lifts."[63]

A bit farther north, passengers look out for the Hole-in-the-Wall, a sea arch carved out of a rocky headland, which hikers on the West Coast Trail can walk under when hiking along the beach at low tide. If the tide is in, canoeists and kayakers sometimes paddle through without touching the sides or the top.

Soon passengers might raise their Brownies to take snaps of one of the great sights of this part of the coast, the magnificent Tsusiat ribbon waterfall, just north of Hole-in-the-Wall. This waterfall, which is 100 ft (30 m) wide, spills the water from Tsusiat Lake down a sheer 80-ft (25-m) cliff onto the beach. "Tsusiat Falls might well be described as the finest natural water cascade on the Island," enthused George Nicholson.[64] Local fishboat skippers can spot the falls from far out to sea and often use the spot as a landmark as they work the waters off the coast. The falls become most spectacular when the tide is high and big swells sweep inshore to envelop them, only to have them magically reappear when the swell recedes. At

Heading north from Clo-oose, the *Princess Maquinna* passed Tsusiat
Falls, where water from Tsusiat Lake cascades into the ocean.
On fine days, passengers could see the falls clearly, if the
ship came close enough. IMAGE COURTESY OF JAMES WHEELER.

such times, though, safety does not allow the *Maquinna* to venture
close enough for sightseeing passengers to witness this spectacular event.

About this time on the voyage, the lunch gong sounds for the two
lunch sittings and passengers once again make their way to the dining room. At this meal, it is quite likely the ship's officers will join
their guests, as they will also do for dinner. Rather than sit together
at one table, the captain sits at the head of one table, while the first
and second officers, the chief engineer and purser, all in full uniform,
sit at the heads of other tables. This custom connects the passengers
and tourists with the crew, and a familiarity and friendship grows
with each trip. The officers also find time, in good weather, to promote deck games such as quoits and shuffleboard, and take time to

point out places of interest, landmarks and the many historical spots along the coast.

A typical lunch menu begins with a choice of hors d'oeuvres of sweet pickles, anchovy toast or chow chow (a green tomato antipasto) followed by clam chowder or fried sole and tartar sauce. Or one might choose a lettuce salad or sliced cucumber or pickled beetroot. Hot dishes included baked pork sausage and mashed potatoes or braised oxtail à la jardinière or grilled loin steak served with fried onions. Cold dishes included roast ribs of beef, boiled ham or head cheese. Vegetables on offer: baked jacket or boiled potatoes and stewed turnips. Sweets to finish: queen pudding, pear pie or compote of apricots followed with imperial Canadian and Kraft cheese with crackers and tea or coffee to wash it all down. All this served by friendly, immaculately dressed waiters who, as Tofino's Bob Wingen recalls, helped young lads like him figure out which utensil to use and when. "We were simply awestruck by the impressive surroundings. When we sat down at the dinner table on the boat there was all this beautiful dinner service laid out with so much cutlery. We were dumbfounded and the stewards would have to teach us how to handle it all. We couldn't afford all those knives and forks at our house."[65]

Some 2.7 nautical miles (5 km) farther north the ship passes the precipitous Valencia Bluffs, where the ill-fated SS *Valencia* foundered in 1906. Pachena Lighthouse, built in 1908 as a result of the tragedy, sits atop the cliffs nearby and possesses the most powerful light on the Pacific Northwest coast, visible for 30 nautical miles (56 km) out to sea on a clear night, and always the first light seen by mariners approaching this part of the coast.

Another 11 nautical miles (20 km) onward, the *Maquinna* rounds Cape Beale and passes its lighthouse, the oldest on the coast, built in 1874. Not quite so powerful as that of Pachena Point, it can be seen 16 nautical miles (30 km) out to sea on a clear night. Rounding the cape, the *Maquinna* steams into the more sheltered waters of Trevor

Passengers enjoying the sunshine on the promenade deck of the *Princess Maquinna* in the 1920s, with Captain Gillam with his back to the camera. IMAGE COURTESY OF THE MOUNT ANGEL ABBEY LIBRARY.

Channel to her next stop at Bamfield, just over 3 nautical miles (6 km) inside the channel.

In good weather, this section of the journey from Port Renfrew to Cape Beale offers some of the most spectacular scenery on the entire trip, and it was this that prompted Superintendent James Troup to explore the idea of selling the *Maquinna*'s west coast journey not just to locals, but to tourists as well.

This was not a new concept. The opportunity to sail up the west coast of BC on an adventurous cruise had fired the imagination of travellers for decades. In 1881 California's Pacific Coast Steamship Company launched the successful Alaska cruise industry with monthly voyages to southeastern Alaska from San Francisco, and was later joined by the Alaska Steamship Company making trips out of Seattle. By 1886 travelling the west coast of Vancouver Island became a tentative recreational event, when the Canadian Pacific Navigation Company advertised in the *Colonist* "... that excursionists could travel to Clayoquot on the little steamer *Maude*."[66] The ss *Tees* also carried some tourists on its voyages, usually sports fishermen and hunters travelling north from Victoria to stay at the hotel at Clayoquot. Soon after the launch of the *Maquinna* in 1913 the Canadian Pacific Steamship Company began cautiously promoting the attractions of the west coast for recreational travellers, something it then did on a much bigger scale in the 1920s and 1930s.

On this summer trip in 1924, the weather has proved remarkably balmy. However, many of the stops made on this stretch of coast would have been impossible in harsher weather, and sightseeing would have been out of the question. The impressive meals would not have been served in such lavish style. Aboard the *Princess Maquinna* in the winter months, and in severe storms, sometimes even the captain and crew faced seasickness. The cooks in the galley did their best for the hardier passengers who were not seasick, and for the crew. They cooked dozens of hard-boiled eggs, which the crew carried in their pockets, eating them when they could, as the ship heaved and tossed for hours, even days, on end.

In March 1934, 17-year-old John Evans paid $3.60 for passage on the *Maquinna* from Victoria to take a job as a helper at the Carmanah Point Lighthouse. His vivid description of the journey north of Port Renfrew, cited in Jan Peterson's book *Journeys*, indicates how passengers coped—or didn't cope—during epic west coast storms. Evans's trip was rough from the very beginning, worsening dramatically as the hours passed:

> Now instead of pitching like a bucking bronco, the *Maquinna* was rolling and pitching. I used to think the water on the east coast of the Island could get rough, but this! I couldn't believe it... Boy, did I get seasick. Then, as if that wasn't enough rough treatment, one of the crew came round and asked us to stand up, so he could tie everything down... My sea-legs just wouldn't hold me steady. In my seasick stupor, I watched the crewman fasten down the furniture. Even the piano was hooked down. By this time I was beginning to wonder what I had gotten myself into... I remember someone telling me I would probably have to continue on up

to Bamfield instead of Carmanah Point as planned, since it was doubtful that anyone would be out to meet the *Maquinna* due to the stormy weather. They told me that I would be taken back to Carmanah Point Lighthouse by lifeboat. This new arrangement didn't appeal to me very much, but there was little I could do about it.

By this time I was so miserably seasick that I decided to go out and get some fresh air. I managed to stagger my way to the door, congratulating myself for not falling flat on my face. The angle at which I had to walk was first up, then down, at which time I fell against the door. I waited until the ship righted herself again, then opened the door. The sight that met my eyes was terrifying. All I could see was a mountain of water! I'm sure it must have been fifty feet high. Luckily one of the crewmen came and grabbed me or I would probably have been washed overboard. He warned me not to open the door again.[67]

All this happened before Evans arrived in Clo-oose, where he managed to survive the dugout trip to the beach and eventually make his way to the light station at Carmanah, where he remained for a year.

On December 30, 1931, the *Daily Colonist* reported that storms raging along the coast had delayed the *Princess Maquinna* at least twenty-four hours in reaching the northern stops on her route, so no one there received mail or Christmas supplies on time. But the newspaper pointed out that "Worse off still were the settlers living at Clo-oose, Carmanah, Hesquiaht, Estevan and Lennard Island, for at all these points Maquinna was unable to call, and in all probability will not be able to do so on the southbound trip either, so great are the seas."[68]

Four years later, in another legendary storm, with Captain "Red" Thompson in command, the *Maquinna* left the shelter of Victoria harbour on December 22, 1935, and headed out into hurricane force winds of up 110 mph (177 kph). The storm had stripped a roof from

The *Princess Maquinna* steaming out of Vancouver Harbour
on her way to Victoria to resume her scheduled run on
the west coast of Vancouver Island. ROBERT D. TURNER PHOTO.

a house in Victoria and left the city without electricity for hours.
Thompson bypassed Clo-oose, and when he reached Cape Beale
at the entrance to Barkley Sound, the going became really tough.
According to the *Colonist*:

> Captain Thompson braced himself in the wheelhouse and nursed
> his gamely struggling ship through the holocaust. He had to fight it
> out as there was no place to run for shelter. In every series of seas,
> there is always a bad one, which reaches higher than the others,
> hoping to claim a victim. Thompson had his ship snugly battened
> down and everyone aboard was warned to have a secure hold. He
> also took the precaution of ordering all his seamen and engineers—
> save one in the engine room—to leave the lower decks. When he
> saw the sea coming he blew the whistle for all hands to brace for
> the onslaught. Then came the big sea which towered over the
> *Maquinna* and Thompson watched it tumble over his ship, tossing
> her almost on her beam ends. Would she come out of it?[69]

She did. Slowly the bow of the *Maquinna* rose to the surface and the rest of the ship emerged. A quick check of the vessel found she was still sound and little water had remained on board. But the freight deck was a shambles. Christmas presents, which had been ordered by mail, and consignments of liquor, turkeys, oranges and other edibles had been strewn amid the heavier freight, all of which had shifted. All crockery in the galley had been smashed and anything that wasn't bolted in place careened around with the roll of the ship. The piano broke her moorings and smashed against the side of the ship. Thompson eventually eased the ship into Bamfield where it took eight hawsers to secure her to the dock.

According to long-time Tofino resident Bob Wingen, who made his first of many trips on the *Maquinna* as a week-old baby in 1926, when his mother brought him back home from Victoria: "They had a nurse on the *Maquinna*, and she was a terrific person. If you were coming and going from hospital she would put you in a stateroom and look after you. But the stewards looked after those who were seasick and there were lots of buckets aboard for people to be seasick into." Bob worked with boats all his life, at his father's (and later his own) boatyard in Tofino. "The *Princess Maquinna* rolled a lot but you never had to be afraid of her. There were times when the captains had to heave to for tides, but she was a very good sea-boat."[70]

As the *Maquinna* nears Bamfield on this journey in 1924, Captain Gillam swings his ship well out into Trevor Channel so he can guide his vessel straight into Bamfield Inlet to dock in front of the cable station. Gillam liked to load as much heavy cargo into his forward hold as he could so that his ship's bow rode "down by the head," which now helps him make the tricky approach to the dock. "The entrance to Grappler Creek [Bamfield Inlet], on which the cable station stood," wrote Gus Sivertz in an article in the *Victoria Times*, "requires a vessel to make an acute right-hand turn or to come in after standing well out off shore and making a wide sweep, through the mouth of Barkley Sound, which could be dirty. With his ship deeper by the bows

Capt. Gillam would just give the rudder a sharp kick and she would turn sharply on her nose and then straighten out for the landing."[71]

As the *Maquinna* enters Bamfield Harbour the ship's whistle sounds—"the most welcome sound on the West Coast," writes Bruce Scott. "Her whistle was unmistakable. It had a pitch all its own and almost invariably faltered on the last note of her 'entering port' signal. Like a young boy's voice, it always broke and ended in a high falsetto."[72] On the port side, the passengers' eyes are transfixed by the imposing building dominating the inlet. There, well above Bamfield's waterfront, stands the Trans-Pacific Cable Station building, the biggest building on the whole west coast—which, for sixty years, played an all-important role in international communications.

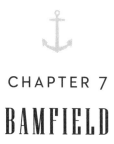

CHAPTER 7

BAMFIELD

I N 1879 renowned inventor and chief engineer of the Canadian
Pacific Railway Sir Sandford Fleming put forward an extraordinary plan. He proposed that the British Empire should connect
its farthest-flung colonies by establishing an empire-wide telegraph cable network. Existing telegraph cable lines already stretched
from Britain to North America under the Atlantic Ocean and across
Canada. Fleming now wanted to add a 4,000-mile (6,430-km)
Trans-Pacific Cable extending all the way from Canada to Fiji, Australia and New Zealand. Because maps at that time usually depicted
the countries of the British Empire in red, the new line bore the
name "All Red Line," signifying it was all-British and that in time of
war, messages sent would be secure.

On November 1, 1902, Fleming's vision became a reality, when
the Trans-Pacific Cable linked Bamfield, on Vancouver Island's west
coast, with the telegraph station on Fanning Island, a small coral
atoll in the mid-Pacific Ocean about 900 miles (1,450 km) south
of Hawaii. From Fanning Island, another line connected to Sydney,
Australia, and to Auckland, New Zealand.

In 1901 the cable company built a three-storey timber building,
which resembled a Canadian Pacific railway hotel, to house the telegraph equipment and the twenty operators transmitting messages
on the All Red Line. BC's most famous architect, Francis Mawson

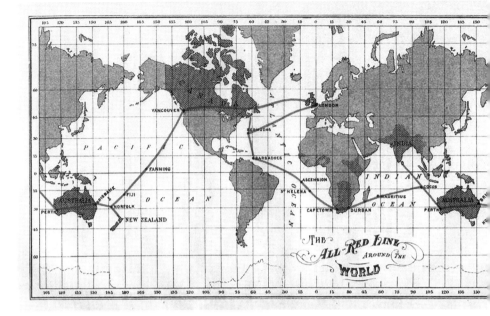

The route of the All Red Line telegraphic cable system
as completed. IMAGE COURTESY OF WIKIMEDIA COMMONS.

Rattenbury, who had designed the Empress Hotel, the BC Legislature and the CPR shipping terminal on Belleville Street in Victoria, drew up the plans for the telegraph station. The building contained about fifty rooms, including a fine dining room with view windows, and amenities such as a billiard hall, a library with three thousand books and a music room. The west coast of Vancouver Island had never seen the like of this palatial structure. Later, in 1926, the company added a new concrete building below the original building to house new technology and allow the twinning of the undersea cables. The ugly building was nicknamed "Alcatraz" by locals.

The scrappy little settlement of Bamfield was established in 1901 when James Budge McKay built the first house there, a boarding establishment with ten bedrooms, a dining room and a store to accommodate workers building the Cable Station. Some fishermen and their families soon joined him in the protected harbour, not expecting that their pretty, isolated village would soon gain international renown because of the Trans-Pacific Cable.

The village of Bamfield derived its name from William "Eddy" Banfield (so spelled) who came to the area in 1849 as one of the west coast's earliest traders. In 1859 he established himself as the first white settler in Barkley Sound when he took up land on Rance Island in Bamfield Inlet, having purchased it from the Huu-ay-aht people for "six blankets, some beans and molasses."[73] In 1861 Governor Douglas appointed him government agent and Indian agent for Barkley Sound. Only a year later, Banfield drowned under suspicious circumstances. Over the years the name "Banfield" became "Bamfield" through common usage.

In 1921 Australian Bruce Scott answered an advertisement in the *Sydney Morning Herald* for "boys fifteen years of age to learn submarine telegraphy and work overseas," and after being trained as a telegraph operator, and having served at various telegraph stations in the Pacific, in 1930 he found himself posted to the Trans-Pacific Station at Bamfield. He would work there for thirty years and came to love the west coast, writing four books, not just about his working life but about shipwrecks, peoples of the coast and Bamfield itself.

In his book *Gentlemen on Imperial Service,* Scott explains that as time passed, the station expanded:

There were also twelve houses and two apartments for married staff; all fully furnished with rugs and carpets, bed-linen and blankets, crockery, cutlery and kitchen utensils—all of which were maintained and replaced when necessary. Accommodation was rent-free and considered to be an isolation bonus. The houses were maintained by a carpenter and outside staff. Laundry and cooking was done by the Chinese laundrymen at a nominal cost ...[74]

Outdoor recreation included tennis on concrete tennis courts, hiking on forest trails, swimming on ocean beaches, salmon fishing, hunting game and ducks, and photography. For indoor recreation there was a dance hall equipped with a stage for amateur theatricals and concerts, and a cinema for movies. Life on the station compared to living at a country club.[75]

The basement at the station provided accommodation for a dozen Chinese men, half of whom would act as servants while the remainder did maintenance work on the property. "You know those poor Chinamen, they were paid slave wages," recalls Bamfield's Johnnie Vanden Wouwer. "That's why they had Chinamen: they were the only ones that would stick it out. But the manager knew better than to boss them. They went at their own speed and that was it. You couldn't speed them up. But they worked steady, you betcha! They worked eight hour days and in the evening, when their shift was over, they fished cod at the floats there, rock cod."[76]

On October 31, 1902, in the first message transmitted on the new All Red Line, the Fijian people sent greetings to King Edward VII in London. "It seemed strange that these islands, so remote, so recently occupied by cannibals, should be the first to transmit, through the newly completed Pacific Cable, a message of respectful homage to the Sovereign of the Great British Empire," effused Sir Sandford Fleming in an interview after the event. "The fact is significant. Is it not another indication that the civilization of the human family is steadily advancing? In this relation we are reminded that, in the British Islands, in that part of the earth where the Fiji message was received by the King, the inhabitants, now highly civilized, were, a few centuries back, a race of painted savages."[77]

The telegraph operators relayed Morse code messages at a rate of 24 words or 120 letters per minute, an easy speed for a capable operator to transmit and to read, and 334,560 words could be moved daily in each direction through the Bamfield station. "Additional space could be saved using abbreviations," says Bruce Scott. "At Christmas time the text of messages containing "Merry Christmas Happy New Year" was abbreviated to MXHNY which the receiving operator typed up in full, thus increasing the capacity of the cable and the speed at which the operator had to work."[78] With re-transmissions, such as those done at Bamfield, it generally took from ten to fourteen hours for a message to be sent around the globe by the various cable stations along the route.

During the years when the cable station dominated the Bamfield skyline and gave it international prominence, only about two hundred people, other than those working at the telegraph facility, resided there, most of them making their living as fishermen. As well, 129 members of the Huu-ay-aht people lived in their main village of Anacla, about 3 miles (5 km) from Bamfield. Their population had numbered in the thousands prior to the arrival of Europeans, but had been decimated by diseases such as smallpox.

With its sheltered harbour and easy proximity to the fishing grounds of the Pacific, thirty or forty boats, mainly trollers, called Bamfield home, and in the summer months as many as a hundred boats might tie up there.

The *Maquinna* generally arrived around midday and stopped for up to two and a half hours on her northbound journey, depending on the weather and the number of stops made since leaving Victoria. She off-loaded supplies for the cable station, and all goods were carried up to the station on a rail trolley pulled by a cable wound round a drum and driven by a gasoline engine. Passengers disembarked to take tours of the imperial cable station and its facilities. This provided the young bachelors who worked there the golden opportunity to escort any young women who happened to be tourists aboard the ship. Jan Peterson attests this in her book *Journeys: Down the Alberni Canal to Barkley Sound* in an interview she did with Bruce Scott. He recalled:

> The coastal steamer called in at Bamfield in the summertime, it was filled with tourists, and the bachelors used to put on their flannels and blazers and go down and eye the human freight, and if possible . . . well the best way to get to know a person or say, a young lady, was to ask them if they wished to see over the Cable Station. Of course everyone wanted to do that, so you had your foot in to a good start. So you saw them over the Cable Station and saw them on board and said well, when you come back they usually hold a dance in the hall at the Cable Station and I'll see you then. So the boat came in on its return journey about four days later, came into

The *Princess Maquinna* in Bamfield, docked below the telegraph station.
IMAGE PN 07209 COURTESY OF THE ALBERNI VALLEY MUSEUM.

Bamfield about midnight and stayed until four or five o'clock in the morning and the bachelors entertained the passengers to a dance at their hall. We had our own orchestra, a five-piece orchestra, and it was an affair which was much looked forward to by the passengers and much enjoyed by the bachelors too.[79]

In his own book *Bamfield Years,* Scott describes how he met his wife at one of these dances. She had come ashore on the "up" trip, and he did not expect the dance on the downward trip to be particularly entertaining, but he went anyway.

When the ship returned, we were having a small dance in the Cable Station library. We gave no thought to her passengers since it was wartime and the station was under military guard to prevent sabotage. No strangers were allowed beyond the wharf unless accompanied by members of the staff.

Halfway through the dance, Captain "Red" Thompson [who succeeded Gillam as the *Maquinna*'s master] entered with a tourist on his arm ... he introduced me to the young lady, whose name was Pauline. It was a case of interest at first sight. We danced and talked until the ship sailed at three o'clock on the morning. I did not see her again until the following year but we corresponded regularly. The following summer she came to Bamfield for a brief holiday and we hiked, boated, swam, took photographs and found that we had many interests in common.[80]

The two married in 1942, moving to one of two cabins Scott had built in a small bay near Aguilar Point at the western entrance of Bamfield Inlet, and which they set about expanding. Bruce ordered all the lumber for the job from a mill in Port Alberni and he expected the *Maquinna* to deliver it at around three in the afternoon. But a delay loading cases of salmon at Kildonan meant the ship didn't arrive until after midnight. Bruce and a friend manoeuvred a borrowed barge alongside the ship:

By the light of the glaring floodlights, the lumber came at us in sling-loads. The mate knew his job and lowered the heavy timbers first. It was frightening the way the stuff came down, but it was well under control and we were never in danger of being hurt. Being amateurs, it took us a few sling-loads before we got the idea of stowing the lumber properly so that the raft didn't tip too much. The winches shirred and hissed steam as sling-load after sling-load came down. There seemed to be no end to the amount of lumber. The raft settled deeper and deeper until it was a foot under water and pieces of lumber began to drift away on the tide. I shouted at the mate and asked him how much more there was. "Quite a lot," he said, so I told him to put the rest on the dock and I would collect it at some future date.[81]

Scott and his friends towed the barge to the bay where the house would be erected and after unloading the materials construction began. The Scotts would live in their refurbished house for many years until they moved to Victoria in the winter months, and later they ran Aguilar House, as they named it, as a bed and breakfast during the summer months. They eventually sold it in 1971.

In 1959, after fifty-nine years of service, the Bamfield Trans-Pacific Station closed, with the relay station moving to Port Alberni.

In mid- to late afternoon on her northbound trip in 1924, with all cargo for Bamfield off-loaded and new passengers welcomed aboard, many of them bound for the next major stop at Port Alberni, the *Maquinna* backs out from the dock into Trevor Channel. She turns eastward into the Alberni Canal, at 30 miles (50 km) the longest inlet on the west coast. In 1931 this would be renamed Alberni Inlet, "because of fears shipping companies would think it was a man-made canal requiring fees."[82] Next stop will be Kildonan, 14 miles (22.5 km) away in Uchucklesit Inlet. Once the *Maquinna* turns into Uchucklesit Inlet the passengers, depending on the time of year, begin smelling the rancid, oily stench emitted by the pilchard reduction plant here, the biggest such facility on all of Vancouver Island's west coast.

CHAPTER 8

SHELTERED WATERS

I N 1917 millions of pilchards (*Sardinops caeruleus*, a member of the sardine family) mysteriously appeared off the west coast of Vancouver Island. Although their usual range is the waters off California, Indigenous people of British Columbia knew of their existence through oral history, which spoke of an oily fish that appeared intermittently over the years. Local non-Indigenous fishermen, however, had not encountered these fish for a generation, and were stunned at their arrival and the sheer numbers of them. Their sudden reappearance, which was to last about thirty years, seems to have been associated with a slight increase in ocean temperature in the region. The pilchards filled the inlets up and down the west coast of Vancouver Island in massive schools. In his memoirs Tofino's Mike Hamilton writes: "There were literally millions of tons of them. The Sound [Clayoquot] teemed with them. They made a sight to be remembered when after dark one could stand in the bow of a power boat and watch the phosphorescent millions hastening out of the way."[83] Eleanor Hancock, in *Salt Chuck Stories from Vancouver Island's West Coast* described them as "bubbling silvery carpets in the inlets."[84]

When the first pilchards arrived, a few salmon canneries on the coast tried to process and can them using the same methods they employed to can salmon. Customers found the pilchards unappetizing and overly oily, so the canneries began reducing (boiling down) the pilchards, extracting the oil and then drying the remains for fish meal. Each ton of fish produced 45 gallons of oil, a product used in making soap, paint, varnish, printing ink, cosmetics, salad dressings, shortening and margarine, as well as a treatment for leather. Farmers used the fish meal as a potent fertilizer or fed it to their cattle and poultry.

Before long, canneries couldn't cope with the quantities of pilchards being caught. Seine boats averaged 50 to 200 tons with each "set" of their nets, occasionally reporting 500 tons being hauled onto one boat. To process this astounding volume of fish, by the mid-1920s, twenty-six reduction plants sprang up on the west coast of Vancouver Island, all located in the 100 miles (160 km) between Barkley Sound and Kyuquot. Construction costs for each plant could reach as much as $250,000. "Suitable sites were at a premium," says George Nicholson in *Vancouver Island's West Coast,* "requiring good penetration for pile driving, shelter for boats and docks, and above all a plentiful water supply. Construction crews could ask any price to build the reduction plants. Victoria and Vancouver shipyards worked night and day building seine boats and scows, while fishing companies vied with one another in a mad scramble to cash in on the bonanza."[85] These reduction plants employed thousands of workers, and kept a fleet of two hundred seiners, tugs and scows busy during the four-and-a-half month season when the fish stayed in the inlets. According to Earl Marsh in his *West Coast of Vancouver Island*: "The business grew so rapidly that in 1928 there were 22 plants in operation, consuming 80,500 tons of fish, the value of which landed at the plants being $2,563,000, which produced 3,995,860 gallons of oil, which was worth about 40 to 45 cents per gallon to the producer, and in addition 14,000 tons of fish meal."[86]

The *Princess Maquinna* became an essential link in the pilchard industry. With so much oil and fish meal being created, the pilchard plants required regular and reliable transport for their products. The *Maquinna*'s cargo holds fairly bulged to overflowing on her run southbound as she called in to these busy plants and loaded up, carrying the oil and fish meal to Victoria for trans-shipment. As

Bamfield's Johnnie Vanden Wouwer attested: "In the summer, the *Maquinna* would load on all this herring meal and pilchard meal instead of going back down [to Victoria] empty. It made great fertilizer (and animal feed), so that paid off for them. The pilchard oil was used as paint. Real thick it was. I remember Randal painted the hospital dwelling with it. You just mixed some coloring in it and that stayed on there for years and years, but there sure was a stink to it for weeks after, especially in the sun!"[87] While the *Maquinna* profited from carrying meal and oil to Victoria, the smells from the reduction plants tested the sensibilities of the *Maquinna*'s passengers. They would wake up in their cabins and know by the smell that the ship was approaching one of the reduction plants on the coast.

Heading up the Alberni Canal from Bamfield the *Maquinna* could potentially call at nine locations: the Indigenous village cannery and logging operations at Sarita Bay; the cannery and saltery at San Mateo; the settlements at McCallum and Ritherdon Bays; the cannery at Kildonan; the village at Green Cove; the logging camp at Underwood Cove; the settlement at Croll Cove; and finally Port Alberni itself. She seldom called at all these places on any one trip, only stopping "when business offered."[88]

The BC Packers fish plant at Kildonan, where the *Maquinna* stopped on both her northbound and southbound journeys, was the biggest fish-processing plant on the west coast in the 1920s. Fish packers from the entire west coast brought salmon to this plant to be canned, and it also processed pilchards and herring. An added bonus for fishermen was the large cold-storage plant, which made ice for the many fishboats and fish packers.

Originally called Uchucklesaht when the Alberni Packing Company built the plant in 1903, the Scottish-born Wallace brothers changed its name to Kildonan, after their home in Scotland, when they purchased the plant in 1911. By the 1920s Kildonan had become a self-contained community, with a store, cookhouse, bunkhouses for both men and women, a recreation hall, its own electric light plant, water and sewage systems, and a school for the employees'

A major fish-processing plant on the west coast in the 1920s, the Kildonan Cannery in Uchucklesaht Inlet developed into a small community, with a store, cookhouse, bunkhouses for men and women, a recreation hall, its own electric light, water and sewage systems, and an ice-making plant.

IMAGE D-00594-141 COURTESY OF THE ROYAL BC MUSEUM.

children. Many local Indigenous women from the nearby Uchucklesaht village worked there during the summer. As well, many Chinese workers arrived each season, living in their separate "China House" at the cannery, where they did their own cooking. Indigenous women and Chinese men played a central role in all west coast canneries and reduction plants; the industry would have experienced great difficulty operating effectively without them. In the 1920s the fishing industry in British Columbia employed twenty thousand people and generated millions of dollars for the provincial economy.

Having arrived at Kildonan around 5 or 6 p.m. the *Maquinna* takes as long as two to two and a half hours to unload goods and load her cargo at the cannery. Then she casts off and backs into Uchucklesit Inlet, and continues her journey up the Alberni Canal.

On a summer evening this next part of the journey proves a delight for the *Maquinna*'s passengers and the calm waters come as a welcome relief after the exposed waters of the open Pacific. Tofino's Tony Guppy offers a lovely description of the trip down the canal:

The heavily timbered shoreline and islands that we sailed past could hardly be matched anywhere in the world for scenic beauty. Clear mountain streams cascaded like jeweled necklaces down the steep hillsides and rocky cliffs. Molded and carved by volcanic and ice age activity, this rugged Pacific coast was wonderfully formed, with long deep inlets of water reaching far into the mountains. Loggers had built wooden flues in some of the mountain streams to carry the huge logs down the perilous slopes to the sea. To see the logs come crashing down from these heights like huge arrows from the clouds was something to behold! The loggers working on these mountain slopes would have appeared like tiny insects to people watching from the ship below. These were the pioneer woodsmen who harvested the trees that supplied the numerous sawmills in operation along this coast. Hand-loggers they were called. Their methods had to be innovative and highly adaptive in order to log in the dense forests that covered this rugged mountainous terrain.[89]

In late evening, the *Maquinna* arrives at the largest town on the west coast, Port Alberni. Settlers began to arrive in the area when Captain Edward Stamp built a sawmill here in 1860 "... erected in a most solid fashion, and at a heavy outlay, by English labourers, and with English machinery."[90] Although the mill did well for a number of years, it eventually closed because of a lack of timber, which seems odd given the abundance of trees lining the sides of the canal and on the mountains behind. But in those early days of hand logging, before steam- and gasoline-driven machinery, most of the timber remained inaccessible except along the fringes of the coastline. Later, when mechanized logging practices developed, the huge trees on the upper slopes became easier to harvest.

In 1863 Edward Stamp left Port Alberni for Burrard Inlet, Vancouver's harbour, where he set up another sawmill, Hastings Mill. The settlement that grew around the mill eventually grew to become the city of Vancouver. His chief forester, Jeremiah (Jerry) Rogers, accompanied him and logged in an area locally called Jerry's Cove, more familiarly known today as "Jericho," now a sought-after area of the city.

Though this first Port Alberni enterprise did not live up to expectations, traders, missionaries, prospectors, fishermen and farmers slowly began to put down roots at the eastern end of the canal, and a small town emerged. In 1892, the first pulp mill in the province opened there but since "it made paper from rags rather than wood,"[91] this unlikely venture closed in 1896. Another fifty years would pass before Bloedel, Stewart and Welch opened a modern pulp and paper mill—using wood chips—in 1946. This became the town's main economic engine for many decades, and its main source of employment.

Port Alberni differed from all the other settlements on the west coast served by the *Maquinna* in that it had optional means of travel, other than by water. In 1886 a road, and by 1911 a railway, linked the community to Parksville and Nanaimo on the east side of the island. Long before settlement, the Indigenous peoples followed their own trails through the mountains of central Vancouver Island in order to trade with First Nations on the other side. Some early settlers used those existing trails to make their way over "the Hump," as the locals call the highest point of the pass through the mountains immediately east of Port Alberni. Travelling from Port Alberni to Nanaimo by train linked westcoasters to an easy boat connection down the Gulf of Georgia to Vancouver and the Lower Mainland. Because of this, Port Alberni became a transportation hub for many on the outer coast. People living in remote communities along the coast, as well as local businesses requiring goods from the Lower Mainland, often had those goods delivered to Port Alberni and then transported on the *Maquinna*, making this a busy stop for the ship. Port Alberni also possessed a modern hospital that took patients from isolated settlements on the coast, with the faithful *Maquinna* often acting as a hospital ship to transport the sick and injured.

After two hours of loading and unloading goods and passengers, the *Maquinna* sets off back down the Alberni Canal, making stops in the dark. This calls for careful navigation. Years later, on the night of January 18, 1934, Captain Robert "Red" Thompson chose to remain at the dock in Port Alberni because of the heavy fog that the ship had encountered on its journey up the Alberni Inlet (as it had been called since 1931) the previous evening. With the weather clearing, at 4:44 a.m. First Officer William "Black" Thompson, in charge of the bridge, eased the ship away from the dock, ordering the engine room to proceed at half speed out of the harbour. While gingerly making her way in the darkness, at 4:52 a.m. the *Maquinna* acknowledged a whistle blast from the MV *Mirrabooka*, a Swedish ship off her port bow, and changed course one degree. Almost immediately after changing course, First Officer Thompson and the lookout at the bow simultaneously spotted the silhouette of a dark object lying dead ahead with no lights showing. Thompson immediately ordered the engines full astern but the *Maquinna* struck the SS *Masunda*, an anchored, 5,250-ton British steamer from Glasgow, three times the size of the *Maquinna*. Despite having put the engines in reverse the *Maquinna* hit the *Masunda* in the bow area, causing considerable damage to both vessels.

After assessing the damage, the *Maquinna* set sail for Victoria at 5:04 a.m., arriving in Victoria at 8 pm. A few days later she was hauled out at the Victoria Machinery Depot where repairs costing $16,000 took place over the next twenty days. The CPR sued the owners of the *Masunda* for damages and at a trial held at the Royal Court of Justice in London on October 10, 1934, Justice Bateson, relying only on the written evidence and witness affidavits, found against the company stating that: "I have come to the conclusion that the vessel had her lights properly exhibited and burning brightly and that the 'Princess Maquinna' is responsible for the accident."[92] Yarrow's Shipyard repaired the *Masunda* at a cost of $24,929, taking twenty days to accomplish the task. Needless to say the CPR was not happy with the judgement but, on the advice of counsel, decided against appealing.

Alder Bloom, a young lad from Saskatchewan who travelled on the *Maquinna* on a rainy August night in the 1920s, eloquently described the return journey down the inlet in an article he wrote:

> I stood on the deck at midnight as the ship left the dock, watching the Port Alberni lights disappear in the gloom. The water was smooth in Alberni Inlet, and the ship made a pleasant swishing sound as it moved along through the dark. I could see the shape of the tall, steep mountains on both sides of the Inlet, starting at the water's edge and reaching to the sky. I climbed into my bunk and slept the sleep of the innocent... The *Maquinna* had three or four stops in Barkley Sound. The main one was Kildonan, the BC Packers fish plant... BC Packers had another reduction plant not far away at Ecoole, and Nelson Brothers had a reduction plant at Toquart. This was my first sight of fish plants and I wasn't much impressed. But if the shore plants, with their white-washed, board-and-batten walls and rusty, galvanized iron roofs, weren't much to look at, the fish boats were another story. They were kept in good shape, well painted and clean, and looked ready to take on the West Coast storms.[93]

Occasionally, on her return journey down the Alberni Inlet, the *Maquinna* might carry a load of coal that had come by train to Port Alberni from the coal mines around Nanaimo, and sometimes she carried lumber to be off-loaded at Bamfield. Long time Bamfield resident Johnnie Vanden Wouwer recalled:

The coal [for the Bamfield Cable Station] came from Nanaimo on the *Maquinna.* She would stay all afternoon unloading the fifty tons from the forward hold. That was all they had was the forward hold, you see. The fifty tons would put her down quite a bit and after they were through, she'd be up by about two feet ... There'd be fifty tons of coal on the dock, in a pile about 20 feet high, that the Chinamen had to load in wheelbarrows and send up in the trolley, which took about ½ an hour to get to the top. And then they had to unload it into a big bin.[94]

With the coal unloaded the *Maquinna* backs out of Bamfield and steams into Barkley Sound and through the Broken Group of islands where she will make only a few stops as she heads north for Ucluelet, her next major port of call.

⚓

CHAPTER 9

BARKLEY SOUND

W HEN THE GOOD Ship *Princess Maquinna* reaches Chup Point, 2 nautical miles (3.6 km) past the entrance to Uchucklesit Inlet on the north side of the Alberni Canal, she rounds the point and steams northward through the islands of the Broken Group. Her next destination is the small dock at the BC Packers reduction plant at Ecoole. The facility here began as a saltery in 1916 that, a decade later, would become a more profitable pilchard reduction plant. After a brief stop of less than half an hour, the *Maquinna* steers across Imperial Eagle Channel. The passengers now have a brief break from the reek of pilchard reduction plants, but earlier in the *Maquinna*'s career something even worse had awaited at the next stop. The whaling station at Sechart was, until its closure in 1918, one of three whaling facilities the *Maquinna* visited along her route, the others being Cachalot in Kyuquot Sound and at Coal Harbour in Quatsino Sound. Long before the *Maquinna* reached Sechart the stench drifted toward the passengers on board. "The odor was indescribable—we literally gagged,"[95] reported one passenger. The plants employed scores of workers, many of them Chinese and Japanese, who flensed the whales and rendered the blubber into whale oil and fertilizer, canning the meat or "sea beef" for pet food. Transporting these items to Victoria for trans-shipment overseas gave a massive boost to the CPR's bottom line.

Men pose on the carcass of a baleen whale at Sechart whaling station in Barkley Sound. IMAGE COURTESY OF THE MOUNT ANGEL ABBEY LIBRARY.

Opened in 1905 by the Pacific Whaling Company, the Sechart plant and the one at Cachalot between them slaughtered 5,700 whales, the majority of them humpbacks, between 1907 and 1925. "Passengers and crew would disembark for a quick tour, keen to view the great piles of bones and baleen and eager to be photographed alongside the immense carcasses awaiting flensing," wrote Mr. H.W. Brodie, the CPR inspector touring the coast in 1918. He could not quite comprehend this, appalled as he was by "the indescribable stench [that] prevails at the whaling station... and make a large number of people very ill."[96]

After an hour's stop the *Maquinna* continues on to the pilchard plant at Toquart for a typical and uneventful stop before rounding the point at the northern entrance to Barkley Sound, just beyond which she reached the village of Ucluelet, meaning "people with a safe landing place." Protected on the southwest by a narrow peninsula of high ground a couple of miles long, Ucluelet possesses an excellent harbour, about half a mile (800 m) wide and deep enough for coastal freighters.

The Ucluelet First Nations village sits along the east shore of the harbour, as does the Nootka Packing Company's Port Albion reduction plant, and some scattered settlement. On the west side of the bay sits the government wharf and the busy village of Ucluelet, much of the shoreline taken up by docks for fishboats. "The outer ends of the floats were occupied by fish buying stations and a couple of oil barges," writes Al Bloom in his diary. "This was the permanent home of many trollers, the majority of them Japanese. They were an industrious group of people, who kept their boats and their home sites in first class condition. They worked hard and made a good living, even though the best price for fish was thirty or forty cents a pound."[97]

While the *Maquinna* pauses at Ucluelet, the tourists aboard prepare to enjoy a local horticultural delight. Here they can go ashore and visit the "Kew Gardens of the West Coast," a widely renowned four-acre garden established by pioneer horticulturalist George Fraser. Others may choose a different local attraction, and can take a truck ride out to the beaches north of the village, including the magnificent Long Beach, the west coast's most famous strand.

Born in 1854 near Fochabers in Scotland, from the age of 17 George Fraser apprenticed as a gardener at nearby Gordon Castle. After completing a four-year course in horticulture in Edinburgh, and having worked on other large estates in Britain, he immigrated to Canada in 1883. He arrived with his sister in Winnipeg, hoping to own land of his own. After two years, he found the harsh winters not to his liking and moved to Victoria, where he established a successful fruit and vegetable garden. When the city of Victoria commissioned a fellow Scot, John Blair, to design and build Beacon Hill Park, Blair hired Fraser as his foreman. While doing this work, Fraser found time to travel to Ucluelet, and in 1892 he purchased Lot 21, consisting of 236 acres, for $236. Today, Fraser's original landholding accounts for almost half the land in the village of Ucluelet.

In 1894 Fraser left Victoria and settled on his land, where he set to work creating a magnificent garden that would attract worldwide attention (though sadly it does not survive today). Later, his brothers James and William joined him.

Setting about building his garden, Fraser encountered rocky ground and poor soil, but he persevered, undaunted even by the 120 in (3 m) of rain a year. He constructed underground wooden drains to draw the water away, he built his soil by collecting seaweed, fish refuse and cow manure, laboriously transporting these from farther up the inlet on a scow, which he towed behind his rowboat. Over time he began growing fifteen types of heather, adding many varieties of rhododendrons, azaleas, roses, fruit trees, berries, and shrubs of all kinds. He started his plants in rooting beds heated from below with warm smoke that made its way inside a clay-tiled flume from a small wood burning heater in his house. Fraser was a happy and friendly man, and his skills as a fiddler came in handy at community events. He became a beloved and well-known figure in the area, though Fraser's reputation spread far beyond the west coast. He already had a respected record as a grower and landscaper when he came to Ucluelet, and from this unlikely location his fame spread. As his garden matured, and the species he grew multiplied, he created mail-order catalogues. He sent orders far and wide, his plants carefully packed in sphagnum moss, and shipped inside wooden crates he made from driftwood. They all left Ucluelet aboard the *Maquinna*. He even sold plants and shrubs to the CPR to enhance many of the company's gardens. His reputation as a planter is best remembered for his skill in propagating hybrid rhododendrons and azaleas. He corresponded with fellow enthusiasts around the world, shipping plants and pollen to growers in England and the United States. One of his hybrids, *Rhododendron* 'Fraseri,' still grows in world-renowned Kew Gardens in London.

George Fraser *(left)* dressed in non-gardening garb.

PASSENGERS FROM "MAQUI
GOING ON B's TRUCK TO
SEE LONG BEACH.
"MAQUINA" STAYED IN UCLUE
LONG ENOUGH FOR THEM T
GO TO SEE IT.

Basil and Mary Matterson beside their tourist truck. In the 1920s and 1930s they carried tourists from the *Princess Maquinna* out to Long Beach during the ship's stop in Ucluelet. IMAGE COURTESY OF DAL MATTERSON.

The *Princess Maquinna* docked at Ucluelet during World War II.
Note the army tent encampment in the top right corner.
IMAGE COURTESY OF THE UCLUELET AND AREA HISTORICAL SOCIETY.

Fraser warmly welcomed visitors who walked up to his garden from the *Maquinna*. In the spring and summer the ship extended her stay so that passengers could enjoy the gardens in full bloom. Fraser would take them on tours, and when they departed, regardless of whether they bought plants or not, he gave them a bouquet of flowers before they returned to the ship. In 1944 Fraser died, aged 90, and when he was being taken aboard the boat to go to the Port Alberni hospital, from which he would not return, he is reported to have said: "I don't know where I'm going to end up, but it doesn't matter—I've had my heaven here on earth."[98]

In the 1930s, when the *Maquinna* stopped in Ucluelet tourists could board Basil and Mary Matterson's "tour bus"—an open truck with seats built onto the flat bed—and take a 12-mile (20-km) ride over the rough, gravel road connecting Ucluelet with Long Beach, one of Canada's greatest natural attractions. In those days, Long Beach formed part of the route travelled between Tofino and Ucluelet, with cars and trucks motoring along the hard-packed sand. Travellers considered this section the best and smoothest part of the whole journey as the road on either side of Long Beach often proved impassible. Between 1942 and 1944, during World War II, nearly a thousand air force personnel served at the amphibious air base established in Ucluelet. Stranraer and Shark float planes from the base patrolled the west coast looking for enemy submarines, and for any signs of a Japanese invasion fleet. It proved a lonely existence for the young men stationed there, and when they received forty-eight-hour leaves, every three or six months, they would make the long, multistage trip to Vancouver. First they had to travel to Port Alberni on the *Maquinna, Lady Rose* or *Uchuck*, then take the train to Nanaimo, where they boarded the CP ferry to Vancouver, arriving late in the afternoon. The return trip by ferry and train landed them back in Port Alberni just after midnight the following day, where some might take a room in the Somass Hotel while waiting for the *Lady Rose* or *Uchuck* to depart in the early morning. Five hours later they reached Ucluelet, where they could reminisce for the next several months about their short but exhilarating time spent partying in Vancouver.

With her passengers back on board, the *Maquinna* unties and rounds Amphitrite Point—named for Poseidon's wife in Greek mythology. The lighthouse on the point, built in 1906, resulted because of the tragic sinking of the three-masted steel-hulled barque *Pass of Metford*. On Christmas Day 1905 the vessel foundered on the treacherous rocks lying just offshore, with a loss of thirty-five lives.

After enjoying the calmer waters of Alberni Inlet, Barkley Sound and Ucluelet's protected harbour, the passengers must now brace themselves. Once again, they are heading into the powerful swells of the open Pacific. The waves come at them unimpeded, across some 6,000 miles (nearly 10,000 km) of open ocean, all the way from Asia. Even if the weather appears sunny and windless, the swells driven by storms farther out in the Pacific still pack a wallop. Johnnie Vanden Wouwer recalled one trip from Bamfield to Tofino: "By gosh there was a big storm! When we got round Amphitrite, Dad was just about all in. Oh, seasick! It seemed to be taking forever and ever to get to Lennard Island in that big swell and she had a full load, too. I was throwin' up and I could hear the propeller come half out of the water and what a crash it would make when it came down! And that Jenny Reef seemed awful close."[99]

Ray Jones, who lived in Port Alice and who travelled on the *Maquinna* from the time he was 7 years old, could relate to this. During one particular storm when he was very young, "the water churned over the tip-tilting decks and nothing but green water could be seen through the portholes. Everyone was directed to stay in their staterooms. For me as a child, it was remarkable to see a steward with arms and legs wrapped around a pole, trying to stay upright, and even more remarkable to see my mother holding a teapot up at the dining room table in the saloon as the crockery crashed to the floor. 'Oh son, we're going to drown,' she cried. But we didn't. The *Maquinna* was more than equal to such storms."[100]

And so she sturdily plows ahead through the swells, with passengers now looking forward to their next major stop, Tofino. First, though, they will pass near to the location where the *Maquinna* met her greatest challenge, in a storm some years earlier, when not even Captain Gillam could succeed in his brave efforts to rescue a foundering ship.

CHAPTER 10

SHIPWRECK AND
SAFE HARBOUR

I N OCTOBER 1915, only two years after the *Princess Maquinna*
began her regular runs up and down the west coast of Vancouver
Island, she ran into a particularly powerful storm. Fatefully, so did
the three-masted Chilean ship *Carelmapu,* in ballast from Hawaii
and bound for Puget Sound to pick up a load of lumber. Normally,
the two ships should not have come near each other, but in such a
storm, anything could happen.

On October 18, the *Carelmapu* reached the entrance of the Strait
of Juan de Fuca, where her captain, Fernando Desolmes, fired a suc-
cession of five flares requesting a tug to tow his ship into port. While
waiting all day for a tow, a strong southeast gale, packing winds of
75 to 80 knots, began driving the ship northwards up the west coast.
Desolmes shortened sail, trying to hold her, but the next day, near
Pachena Point at the entrance to Barkley Sound, a vicious blast blew
out most of his ship's sails. This forced him to hoist distress signals as
the wind continued to drive his thirty-eight-year-old ship up the coast
until it reached Lennard Island near the north end of Long Beach.

With his ship's sails in tatters, Desolmes ordered his crew to
throw two anchors into the 240-fathom (440-m) depth of water
in an attempt to hold the ship and prevent her from going onto
nearby Gowlland Rocks. Other members of the crew attempted to

launch a lifeboat, only to have it swamp, hurling the occupants into the breakers.

As the imperilled *Carelmapu* headed toward the rocks, Captain Gillam and the *Princess Maquinna* neared Tofino on their regular voyage southbound on their west coast route. After stopping there, Gillam made the decision to "make a run for it," despite the weather, and continue journeying south. If the gale proved too severe when he reached open water, just past the Lennard Island Lighthouse, he planned to return to the shelter of Tofino until the storm abated. When the *Maquinna*, with fifty passengers aboard, reached Lennard Island at the south end of Templar Channel, where the relatively calm waters of the channel gave way to open ocean, Gillam reported that he could see the sea breaking in a line as far as Cox Point. After consulting with his officers, he decided to head back to Tofino and wait out the storm rather than endanger his ship and passengers. Before he turned his vessel around, however, a lookout spotted the *Carelmapu* some distance offshore flying flags upside down, the international distress signal. "Then we had no alternative but to keep on in the face of anything, as we knew that lives were in danger," Gillam later told the *Victoria Daily Colonist*.[101]

With waves breaking over the pilot house and spray flying over the masthead, Gillam steered the *Maquinna* to within 150 yards (140 m) of the stricken ship. "*Maquinna* handled splendidly, and at full speed she plunged into the tremendous seas, first perched on the crest of a great wave and then down in the abyss, skimming over the frenzied water like a duck,"[102] Gillam reported. He then turned his ship seaward into the mountainous Pacific waves and set his anchor. With the ship's engines turning at half revolutions to hold her into the waves, he ordered oil poured overboard from the fuel tanks to help calm the raging seas. As the sea calmed slightly due to the oil, the Chileans lowered seven men into a second lifeboat—the first having foundered—and they began valiantly rowing toward the *Maquinna*. But the strength of the waves exhausted the rowers before they could reach a lifeline thrown to them from the stern of the *Maquinna*, and

The *Carelmapu* in distress, her sails ripped to shreds. This
photograph was taken by a passenger aboard the *Princess
Maquinna* during her attempted rescue of the stricken vessel.

the small boat overturned, throwing its occupants into the churning
sea. None survived. Some of the crew of the *Maquinna* offered to try
launching one of her lifeboats in an attempt to save them but Captain Gillam, deeming it too dangerous, refused permission.

Suddenly, despite the engines keeping her heading into the
oncoming sea, a massive wave hit the *Maquinna* with such impact
that the winch holding the anchor chain on the forecastle deck began
buckling the deck plates under the strain, and the steel decking
began to lift. The same wave tore the *Carelmapu* from her anchors,
leaving her entirely at the mercy of the storm, heading toward Gowlland Rocks. Realizing the hopelessness of the situation, Gillam then
ordered First Mate C.P. Kinney to go to the forecastle deck and cut
the *Maquinna*'s anchor chain with a hacksaw. Kinney had to be
lashed down and held by crewman Harry Hamilton to prevent him
being washed overboard as he laboured to cut the huge anchor chain.
It took Kinney an hour and a half to cut through the iron chain-link,

1.5 in (4 cm) thick, before the anchor let go, at which point Gilliam reluctantly pointed the *Maquinna* out to sea, leaving the *Carelmapu* to her doom in Schooner Cove. As he headed out to sea Gilliam looked back to see Desolmes waving a despairing farewell, and the *Maquinna*'s passengers watched in horror as the mizzen mast of the shipwrecked vessel ripped off, tossing two of the remaining men overboard into the sea. Desolmes released himself from the railing, genuflected, and dropped into the ocean. Against all odds, he made it to shore.

Gillam had done all he could under the perilous circumstances. "Rather than have the bow ripped out of her I ordered the 60 fathoms [110 m] of anchor chain to be severed. With nothing between us and the reefs, I was forced to navigate *Maquinna* out to sea ... I was in charge of a large number of passengers and could not take any more risks. We steamed from there direct for Ucluelet and remained there overnight," Gillam told the *Colonist*. "Never in all my long experience in west coast service have I been called upon to nurse a ship through such terrible seas."[103]

Amazingly, five of the twenty-three-man crew of the *Carelmapu*, including Captain Desolmes, survived the sinking, along with the ship's Great Dane, Nogi. Long Beach settler John Cooper buried eleven of the bodies that eventually washed up on the shore, and later wrote: "Nobody knows where they are but myself." Captain Desolmes and one of the survivors, Rodrigo Diez, stayed at Long Beach with Cooper; the other three went to the hotel at Clayoquot, in care of the Tofino lifeboat crew. "All were in very bad shape," commented Cooper. He adopted Nogi, who wore a brass collar with the name of the ship on it, but two years after being saved "a souvenir hunter shot him for the *Carelmapu*-inscribed brass plate on his collar."[104] The stricken and broken remains of the ship remained on the Gowlland Rocks for many years before storms eventually tore her off the promontory.

The *Carelmapu* incident put the *Princess Maquinna* and Captain Gillam in the public eye as never before. "The gallant skipper has nothing but praise for his officers and members of the crew, but he is very modest in taking any credit himself for the part played by *Princess Maquinna* in stretching out a helping hand to the disabled ship... *Princess Maquinna* did all that was asked of her and Capt Gillam is proud of the vessel and the way in which she handled herself under the prevailing conditions,"[105] declared the *Colonist* newspaper. Sometime after the incident, when the *Carelmapu* survivors reached Victoria on the *Maquinna,* Rodrigo Diez, who spoke English, told a reporter: "The *Maquinna* captain was magnificent. I'll never forget his courage in bringing his ship right into the breakers. I shudder to think of it."[106]

For summertime tourists, steaming north from Ucluelet on our imagined trip in 1924, the desperate peril of the *Carelmapu* may be almost impossible to imagine. Though this section of the trip is in open waters, despite the rolling of the ship, fine weather allows passengers to sit outside on the upper deck in chaise longues, reading and chatting, as they watch the passing scenery. They might even enjoy a game of shuffleboard or quoits on deck. Al Bloom describes a trip on the *Maquinna* from Ucluelet to Tofino:

On leaving the sheltered bay at Ucluelet, the *Maquinna* made a sharp turn to the right and sailed between jagged rocks that looked very dangerous to a landlubber. Waves were breaking on these rocks and sending spray high into the air. The ship began to roll slightly. As we cleared the rocks and turned in a northerly direction again, we were out on the open ocean, and the long Pacific swells caught the ship broadside. She rolled along in great style. To the west, except for a few trollers that kept disappearing in the trough, only to reappear again on top of the giant waves, there was water as far as the eye could see. To the east was the now-famous Long Beach, although it was many years before the road from Alberni would be built and tourists would flock to Pacific Rim Park. In my time, Long Beach was used as a road between Ucluelet and Tofino, and it made a fine speedway, well maintained by the waves. There

People often sported their best clothes when travelling on the
Princess Maquinna. Here Harold Monks plays quoits on the upper
deck in 1921. IMAGE COURTESY OF LOIS WARNER.

were few cars around, and the truck drivers who used the route had
to watch for tides. A breakdown with tides coming in spelled doom
for the truck; it would be sucked down and covered with sand in
short order... Our rolling ride only lasted a couple of hours and
was quite pleasant, but during storms this was a rough stretch to
travel. The waves hit slightly on the stern side and gave the boat an
unpleasant twisting, rolling motion.[107]

After rounding Lennard Island Lighthouse, the vessel turns into Templar Channel. There the ship's officers might point out to interested passengers where the sailing ship *Tonquin* met its end, just off the east coast of Echachis Island, in 1811. The *Tonquin*, owned by John Jacob Astor's Pacific Fur Company, had arrived from Astoria, Oregon, to trade for sea otter furs with the local Tla-o-qui-aht people. For various reasons trading negotiations went catastrophically wrong, angering the Tla-o-qui-aht who attacked the ship, killing all but six of the ship's company. The next day some three or four hundred Tla-o-qui-aht returned to the ship with plunder in mind, but the wounded ship's clerk, James Lewis, who had remained hidden aboard, took drastic action. He lit the nine thousand pounds of gunpowder stored in the *Tonquin's* hold, blowing up the ship and killing himself and over two hundred of the Tla-o-qui-aht aboard.[108] This incident marked the end of the maritime sea otter fur trade, which had flourished since Captain Cook arrived on the west coast in 1778 and which had all but annihilated the sea otter population along the coast.

Rounding Grice Point, the *Maquinna* approaches the village of Tofino, where she always receives a warm-hearted welcome. The whole village turns out on "Boat Day" to greet the ship. As in every community on the coast apart from Port Alberni, no road links this village to the outer world. Work on the road to Ucluelet has been staggering ahead in fits and starts for years, but it is still best described as a rutted path, and won't be completed until 1928. "So the arrival of the *Maquinna* in Tofino, as elsewhere on the coast, is a social and economic highlight like no other…"[109] In her book *Lone Cone*, Dorothy Abraham recalls how the *Maquinna* once unexpectedly arrived in the middle of the Sunday church service. When the congregation heard the whistle they all rushed out and headed for the wharf, leaving the minister preaching to empty pews. Schoolchildren also ran from their classrooms once the whistle sounded.

In 1924, when our imagined voyage takes place, the village of Tofino held a population of just over one hundred Scots, English, Scandinavian and Japanese settlers. The Tla-o-qui-aht village of

Opitsat lay across the harbour, with a population of around one hundred and fifty. By the 1920s, the village of Tofino boasted a lifeboat station, two shops—Towler and Mitchell's, and Elkington's— the St. Columba Anglican church, a school, the Wingen boat yard and machine shop and, about 12 miles (20 km) up Tofino Inlet, the Clayoquot Fish Cannery. Fishboats line the shore in front of the village and when the *Maquinna* docks small boats converge from all over the harbour, and from up the nearby inlets, to collect their mail and parcels, and greet visitors. The Tla-o-qui-aht carvers and weavers sell baskets and carvings to visitors as they disembark.

Ron MacLeod, who was born in Tofino where his father Murdo served as fisheries officer, provides a wonderful description of what the *Maquinna*'s arrival meant to the village:

Mail, freight and passengers were brought into Tofino by a Canadian Pacific steamer, for years the *Princess Maquinna*, on the 3rd, 13th and 23rd of each month. On its return journey to Victoria three days later, it would pick up outgoing passengers, cargo and mail. A $10.50 fare would cover the cost of the two-day trip to the provincial capital, Victoria, if one shared a stateroom ... The officers and many of the deck and engine room crews were Scots from the Hebrides or Orkneys and a young traveller with a name like mine would be shown a great time on the trip. The arrival of the steamer was always an event. Tofino locals and Indians from the villages would gather on the government wharf to catch the excitement of the day: freight and mail unloading; salesmen coming off with their large sample cases and rushing to cover the two general stores in the limited time before the ship sailed on; a host of tourists in summer; travellers to up-coast communities enjoying a brief visit on the dock with friends. Indeed, a veritable feast of new faces and body shapes and sizes on which to make comment. In summer, Indian women would take up station on the wharf and sell woven basketwork, carvings and other artifacts. Up and down the wharf would trundle handcarts carrying newly arrived freight to the two stores.

Harold Monks and Margery (Madge) McCannel, with
Princess Maquinna behind, in dock at Tofino, 1921.
IMAGE COURTESY OF LOIS WARNER.

A hive of activity! How empty the government wharf seemed when
the *Princess Maquinna* pulled out!

Marriages in Tofino were often timed so the newlyweds could
leave on the southbound trip of the *Princess Maquinna*. Celebration
of the rites would be followed by a dinner held in the Community
Hall, the larger of the two halls in the village. Practically everyone in the village would be invited to these events. Money may
have been scarce but the generosity of the community was rich
when it came to getting newlyweds off on the right foot. By midnight, the *Maquinna* would arrive and the couple would board the
vessel under a shower of rice and hearty good wishes for a joyous
honeymoon.[110]

For boat builder Hilmar Wingen, who owned the Tofino Machine
Shop and was renowned for building some of the finest fishboats on
the west coast, the arrival of the *Maquinna* played an integral part
in his business. She transported much-needed supplies and parts

"Shorty" Wright, renowned winch man of the *Princess Maquinna*.
IMAGE P918-05008 COURTESY OF THE VANCOUVER MARITIME MUSEUM.

to him from Victoria. "We would take our truck onto the dock and winch man 'Shorty' Wright would drop the parts right into it," said Hilmar's son, Bob. When the Wingens had a hull ready to accept its engine they would bring it alongside the *Maquinna* and Shorty would drop it right into the hull for them. "Once it was in the right place Dad and our crew would mount it in place. It saved us a whole lot of time and trouble," remembers Bob, who would later own the shop. "Shorty was a past master at loading and unloading. He wasn't very big and you'd wonder how he did it. He was one of a kind. Dad always made sure Shorty got a bottle of Scotch for his efforts."[111]

Tofino didn't have a liquor store in those days and people in the community had to send their orders for whatever they needed down to Port Alberni on the *Maquinna*'s southbound run. On the next trip up coast, all the booze orders came back on a pallet that was lifted off the ship and put into a locked warehouse. "People came and picked their orders off the pallet and nothing was ever taken," remembers Wingen. "A few days later there would be a bottle of rum or the like sitting there that someone hadn't picked up yet, but nobody touched it. Christmas time was a particularly busy time for the *Maquinna* bringing booze to people all up and down the coast."[112]

Johnnie Vanden Wouwer relates how some of the liquor arrived in Bamfield: "About every month the people living next door, they'd get a box of whiskey and a barrel of beer in on the *Maquinna*. Talk about 'roll out the barrel'! They were long-neck bottles, packed in straw, and how they fitted them in there is beyond me. These barrels were darned heavy. I remember him [the neighbour] rolling one up the approach to the house. They were staved barrels, quite thin, especially made for this, you know, because they couldn't hold water. When the bottles were empty, they threw them out the back. There was beer bottles back of the house about six feet thick!"[113]

For Tofino's children the arrival of the *Maquinna* brought unimaginable delight. "All of us kids wanted to catch the rat line," recalls Ken Gibson. "We'd hear the whistle out in the harbour and just ran like heck down to the dock to where the *Maquinna* was coming in." The rat line, with a monkey's paw at the end (a heavy ball of spliced rope shaped like a ball) would be thrown onto the dock by a crewman for the lads on the dock to catch and haul in. Attached to the rat line, the much heavier and robust hawser had to be handled by grown men, but the local lads felt that by catching the rat line they were "bringing the boat in."[114]

Once the boat had been secured, and the gangplank was in place, the children would rush onto the boat heading for the commissary in the main lobby. There they would spend their saved up nickels and dimes buying sweets and comic books to tide them over until the next visit of the *Maquinna*. With candy and reading material secured the children returned to the dock to watch the loading and unloading. Sometimes a car or a truck would swing out onto the dock in a specially made sling, or a cow, or a load of hay, or perhaps a load of furniture. One newlywed couple's furniture arrived with two single beds, causing no end of discussion in the community.

The *Maquinna* seldom ventured up Tofino Inlet past the government dock, although there were exceptions. In its September 30, 1917, issue, the *Colonist* reported the *Princess Maquinna* travelling about 11 nautical miles (20 km) up the inlet to Mosquito Harbour, the site of the failed cedar shingle mill, which had closed in 1907. There she loaded "about 2 million shingles," which she took to Seattle for the Sutton Lumber Company. Before the mill shut, it had shipped most of its product out on the freighter *Earl of Douglas* for sale in New York, but huge piles of shingles were still left on the dock at Mosquito Harbour, and remained there for ten years until the owners arranged for the *Maquinna* to pick them up. On another occasion, according to Tofino resident Ken Gibson, the *Maquinna* made her way up the inlet to the Clayoquot Cannery at Kennedy Falls. Unfortunately, her mast severed the overhead telegraph wire that ran from the cannery to Long Beach. The smaller *Tees* regularly made trips to the cannery prior to the arrival of the *Maquinna* in 1913. Her larger size clearly made the journey up the inlet more challenging.

With passengers and freight off-loaded, the *Maquinna* steams five minutes—the shortest leg of her journey—across Tofino harbour to Clayoquot on Stubbs Island. Clayoquot preceded Tofino as the first European settlement in Clayoquot Sound; a trading post was first established there in 1854. A long sandy beach provided easy and safe canoe access for First Nations people coming to trade their furs. Over time, the trading post gave way to a store, and later a hotel and a long curving wharf, complete with rails and a trolley that carried goods and luggage to and from the ship to the store and hotel. Clayoquot even had a jailhouse and a resident policeman at one time. By the 1920s a settlement of Japanese fisherfolk lived there, one of three such settlements in the area.

As more settlers arrived in the area in the early decades of the twentieth century, Tofino slowly outstripped Clayoquot as the main

The beach at Clayoquot, with a ship (possibly the *Princess Maquinna*) at the long dock in front of the store and hotel. Tram tracks along the dock moved supplies to shore. Ships' passengers could walk the sandy shoreline while cargo crews were busy loading and unloading. FRANK LEONARD PHOTO. IMAGE 16677 COURTESY OF THE VANCOUVER PUBLIC LIBRARY.

commercial centre of the region. However, the *Maquinna* continued to pay short visits to Clayoquot until the very end of her days in the 1950s, serving the hotel and the handful of people still living there.

On the very short leg of the journey between Tofino and Clayoquot the *Maquinna*'s helmsman had to be on his toes, for a number of reasons. First, Tofino Inlet is infamous for its sandbars and shoals, invisible in the days before radar when fog shrouded the area: "the *Princess Maquinna* sometimes had to anchor until the fog lifted because of the sand banks and strong currents that abound in the area."[115] Secondly, and very importantly, the Clayoquot Hotel possessed the only liquor outlet between Port Alberni and Port Alice. "It was a particularly busy place, especially on a Saturday night," wrote Neil Robertson. "If the *Maquinna* was crossing from Tofino to Clayoquot shortly after closing time she had to make her way through an armada of small boats and canoes making their unsteady way back to Tofino."[116]

CHAPTER 11

CLAYOQUOT SOUND

HE NEXT LEG of the *Princess Maquinna*'s northward journey takes her through some 27 nautical miles (50 km) of Clayoquot Sound. This proves to be relatively easy travel because two large islands, Vargas and Flores, and a number of smaller ones, shield the sound from the open Pacific. Clayoquot Sound comprises a labyrinth of inlets and bays, fed by four main rivers, the Bedwell, Moyeha, Megin and Sydney, and many smaller creeks and streams.

To serve the isolated settlers, fish plants, logging shows and mining enterprises, the *Maquinna* makes "boat stops" as she travels up the sound. Often a lone occupant in a rowboat, a small gasboat or a canoe comes out from shore to the side of the ship so crew can offload their mail and goods. "She would often pull into a small float camp or a booming ground and unload loggers' cargo out the side hatches," recalls Bill Moore in BC *Lumberman*. "She had two large iron doors on her sides down near the water's edge, and when these were opened freight could be passed out to waiting hands. It may be the middle of the night in a snowstorm or it might be in a strong tidal inlet. No matter, the captain of the *Maquinna* would hold her in position while the logger or fisherman took his freight off."[117]

By the 1930s, people who owned radios in the remote camps and communities up and down the west coast could determine the approximate time to venture out in their boats to meet the *Maquinna*. Vancouver's *Daily Province* newspaper owned a radio station, CKCD, and its evening newscaster Earle "Mister Good Evening" Kelly would inform westcoasters of the *Maquinna*'s progress so they could time meeting the ship for boat stops. In 1929 Kelly, an Australian of Irish heritage who had been wounded at Gallipoli, arrived in Vancouver and for the next seventeen years read a fifteen-minute-long newscast every evening at 9 p.m., seven days a week. Sartorially elegant, Kelly always delivered his Saturday broadcast standing in front of the microphone, as many other announcers at the time did, wearing impeccable evening clothes. He carefully articulated every word. "He spoke so slowly and formally," remembers Tofino's Marguerite Robertson. "He always said *Clay-oh-quat*—never 'Klakwot'—and Tofino was always *To-fee-no* and Ucluelet was *You-cloo-let*."[118] He always concluded his broadcasts with what he referred to as "the benediction": "'We wish all our listeners, on land, on the water, in the air, in the woods, in the mines, in the lighthouses—and especially my friends on the Good Ship *Maquinna*, now off Cape Beale [or departing Tofino, or wherever] a restful evening.'"[119] Those pronouncements each night provided westcoasters with a reasonably up-to-date idea of where the *Maquinna* was on her journey up or down the coast.

About 2.5 nautical miles (4.5 km) up the sound from Clayoquot, the *Maquinna* makes her next stop, at Kakawis on the west side of Meares Island. Here stands an imposing white building, the Christie Roman Catholic Indian Residential School. Opened in 1900 with just thirteen students, it soon grew to house over one hundred, and would continue operating until 1971. Initially staffed by Benedictine priests and nuns, many of them from Belgium and Switzerland, the school possessed a number of scows and barges, making loading and off-loading somewhat easier than the process at Clo-oose, where canoes were used. However, rough weather could sometimes swamp or overturn these scows. Given the number of students and staff living at the school, sustaining them required large amounts of supplies ranging from building materials to furnishings to food, and the unloading "required careful timing, reasonable tides, and a good

"MR. GOOD-EVENING"

Caricature of Earle Kelly by cartoonist Jack Boothe. The *Province* newspaper, March 25, 1948. IMAGE COURTESY OF THE *PROVINCE*.

deal of assistance. Landing flour was particularly tricky, for once wetted it could not be used—and huge amounts of flour arrived regularly... Deliveries of two tons of flour at a time could arrive at Christie School requiring every available person to swing into action."[120]

Though a Protestant and an Orangeman, Captain Gillam befriended the nuns and priests who ran Christie School, becoming a particular

Christie Residential School at Kakawis on Meares Island, taken
in 1905. The Roman Catholic school operated from 1900 until 1971.

friend of Father Charles Moser. Father Charles had been on the west
coast since 1901, and in his diary often mentions Captain Gillam.
Possibly because of Gillam's friendship, students travelling to and
from the school on the *Maquinna* sometimes slept in staterooms,
despite regulations indicating that such accommodation was for
white passengers only. In 1924, when Father Charles shepherded
a large group of First Nations children to the school aboard the
Maquinna, he recorded in his diary: "I had 29 children to take care of
after leaving the Whaling Station [Cachalot], and at 9 p.m. at Nootka
got four more. The 33 spent the night divided in eleven staterooms.
For fares and rooms I paid the Purser $146.90."[121]

On another occasion, on April 24, 1927, he wrote of children
heading back to their villages from Christie School: "Said Mass at 4
a.m. When we heard the steamer [*Maquinna*] whistle, got baggage
and children ready... I got staterooms for the girls and placed the
boys in the steerage."[122] Steerage usually meant that the children
were put out of the way in one of the cargo holds. "Violet George,
who lived at Nootka, first travelled to Christie School on Meares
Island when she was six years old, with her two older sisters. Her
father paid the fare from Nootka Cannery, and the girls travelled in

the cargo hold, where they stayed for many hours before reaching the school. With no benches provided, they sat on their suitcases; a bucket served as a toilet."[123]

It was the norm for Indigenous travellers to travel outside on the open forward deck in summer or, in winter, in the cargo hold between decks. Though this policy doesn't appear to have been a published regulation originating from head office, a look at the fare schedules reveals it. A CPR document from 1913 listing meal rates states: "Indian and Oriental Deck Class Tickets do not include meals or bunk, and such passengers may be served Second Class meals at a rate of 25 cents per meal."[124] A 1936 Fare Schedule instructs pursers to charge "North American Indian Deck Class ONE HALF the First Class fare between ports when the First Class fare does not include meals and berth and that, where they do include meals and a berth to First Class passengers, they should charge TWO-THIRDS the First Class fare."[125] So, for instance, if an Indigenous person travelled from Port Renfrew to Port Alberni in 1936, with no need for meals, the cost would be half a First Class fare, or $2.20. A 1939 Fare schedule lists fares as: First, Indian and Deck Classes.[126]

In summer the forward deck of the *Maquinna* would be packed with Indigenous people and their possessions as they made their way from their reserves to work at various fish plants, as Bill Moore describes in his article in the *BC Lumberman* in 1977: "The fishing and cannery industry was going great guns in the 1920s and a great deal of the work was done by native Indians. Early each summer on her way north, the *Maquinna* would pick up a few hundred native Indians at various stops along the way and deliver them to the canneries at Rivers Inlet on the northern mainland of BC's coast…these people were herded together on deck and down below, sleeping where they could, and getting their own meals. When the ship was at a dock, they would catch some fish and use their big iron pot to cook the fish—on the beach. The trip took several days to Rivers Inlet and one can only sympathize with the plight of those people."[127] In late summer and early fall Indigenous people also found seasonal

Indigenous people travelled regularly on the *Princess Maquinna*, often en route to various canneries on the west coast. Only allowed to travel "deck class," they settled where they could on the foredeck, often cooking their food on shore at various stops along the way. IMAGE D-06893_141 COURTESY OF THE ROYAL BC MUSEUM.

work in the hops fields of Puyallup County in Washington State, and whole families boarded the *Maquinna* for the trip down to Victoria, where they then took other steamers to their US destinations.

Putting Kakawis behind, the *Maquinna* continues north, then heads west into Calmus Passage, at the north end of Vargas Island, passing Port Gillam on her port side. Named after Captain Gillam when he was captain of the *Tees*, the wharf built here prior to World War I served a group of homesteaders attempting to establish themselves on the island. After most of the men left Vargas to serve in World War I, the settlement failed, and the Port Gillam wharf vanished in a severe winter storm only a year after it had been built. When the need arose, steamers could still make infrequent boat landings there. On the mainland, across from Port Gillam, lies imposing Catface Mountain, so named because the copper deposits in the rock gives it a catlike appearance. The waters off Catface are shallow and treacherous, as Father Charles Moser relates in his diary for December 7, 1923. While travelling south on the *Maquinna:* "Off Catface Mountain steamer touched ground two times, no damage except in the dining room where dishes were hurled to the floor and broken."[128]

Once away from the choppy shallows off Catface, the ship arrives at the large First Nations village of Ahousaht on Flores Island. Ahousaht stands on the west side of the long, narrow Matilda Inlet, with the Marktosis Reserve on the east side, and is the biggest First Nations settlement in Clayoquot Sound, with a population of approximately 200 in the 1920s.[129] A Presbyterian Residential School, established at Ahousaht in 1904, stands only 9 miles (14 km) from the Christie Roman Catholic School at Kakawis, making these the closest residential schools to each other in British Columbia.

Dr. Richard Atleo, Chief Umeek of Ahousaht, recalls the arrival of the *Maquinna* as it neared Ahousaht:

> When the *Princess Maquinna* was approaching Ahousaht, when it was still on the other side of Catface Mountain, you could feel it. You could hear it. This was back when there were no sounds from machinery; when a man could go to the top of the hill and call people to a feast in the traditional way. You could feel it in your body: it's almost imperceptible, but you could feel it. It's gentle, but it's also shocking because of the contrast … A huge machine like that, ploughing the waves, disturbs the environment, sets your heart a-pumping … because it was so quiet normally. It was very dramatic. This would only be true in the summertime, though; in wintertime the waves would be roaring loudly.[130]

Inspector H. Brodie describes what he witnessed on his trip to Ahousaht in 1918, before a dock had been built in the 1920s. "This is a very beautiful spot, the village being on a curved beach. The majority of our Indians disembarked at this point. It is very interesting disembarking them, as they are all handled in dugouts. The

Indians pile into the dugouts, baggage, men, women, children, dogs, pots, pans, etc. etc. Among other things there were small cook stoves, stove pipe, hats, strips of oil cloth and all sorts of paraphernalia. It took about an hour to disembark all the Indians."[131]

By 1921, Ahousaht had become home to the legendary, larger-than-life Gibson family: father William, mother Julia and sons Clarke, Jack, Earson and Gordon. William had been active on the west coast for years before then, harvesting lumber for various markets and encouraging settlement. He built his own sawmill at Ahousaht in 1921, cutting spruce for airplane frames and splitting cedar shakes and shingles. The Gibsons relied on the *Maquinna* to carry their products to market, but with only a small dock unable to accommodate the ship they had to improvise, and in Gibson-like, make-do fashion they did just that, as Gordon describes in his book *Bull of the Woods*:

The *Maquinna* couldn't tie up close to our dock so we would load our shingles on a huge float 50 feet by 140 feet ... then we would tow it out to be anchored about a mile down the bay. We would load the shingles from the float onto the 'tween decks of the *Maquinna*, a good 5 feet up from the water line.

This would take four or five hours, usually at night, by which time we were soaking wet from the rain the salt water or sweat. My father and brothers would make our way home, have a hot meal and fall into bed for a few hours' sleep before starting to operate the mill in the morning. After a few months of towing the float out to the *Maquinna* we decided to secure the raft to the shore, and take a chance that Captain Gillam could bring the *Maquinna* in to us.

We drove in some piles and I reinforced the lashing, putting in stiff-legs—poles about 80 feet long—to keep the float offshore. We used cables that were brought down from an old mine which had started before World War I at the head of Bear River. Fastening 1,000 feet of this cable firmly to the float at each corner, we secured it to stumps on shore. Now as we cut our shingles we were able to pile them on our float ready for shipment eliminating that terrible towing trip. Because the engine in our boat had less than 10 horsepower we had to go down the bay with the tide and sometimes wait for six hours for another tide to make the return trip. Captain Gillam came in to look at our mooring and decided that he would risk bringing the *Maquinna* alongside it. She tied up to this float six times a month for many years, docking three times going north and three more times on her return trip.[132]

In the mid-1920s when the enormous schools of pilchards arrived annually on the coast, sometimes stretching the equivalent of two or three acres under the water, the Gibsons saw an opportunity. They used their pile driver to build foundations and wharves for reduction plants up and down the coast. They also sold lumber from their sawmill to build the reduction plants. In 1926, after seeing the profits being made from the reduction plants they helped to build, they decided to construct their own plant at Ahousaht. That kept them even busier, and financially better off. "We logged and ran our mill in the winter, as well as shipping salt salmon to China, and we went fishing pilchards in summer,"[133] writes Gordon in *Bull of the Woods*.

Amid all this enterprise the young, socially isolated Gibson brothers took full advantage of the opportunity to meet the young lady tourists travelling on the *Maquinna*. "In the summertime the *Maquinna* would bring a group of tourists up the coast, arriving at our place about six in the afternoon. All of us young bucks were tickled to death to take the tourists for a walk to the outside beaches, often building a campfire for a singsong and perhaps stopping for a soak in the hot springs on the way back. Naturally, we were most anxious to escort any of the attractive young ladies. After the walk we took everyone back to our home for coffee and a dance."[134]

In 1933 the pilchards that had been on the west coast for fifteen years almost disappeared. The Gibsons, like many other reduction-plant owners, experienced a severe economic downturn, nearly bankrupting them. It took them a number of years to recover from

Off-loading freight from the *Princess Maquinna* at Ahousaht, 1918.

this financial crisis, but they weathered the storm by taking every opportunity to make money. In 1932 the *Maquinna* needed a new mast and the Gibson brothers were renowned for finding any way to make a buck, so with the CPR offering $100 to procure one, the Gibsons jumped at the opportunity. "That was a huge sum of money for us and we immediately contracted to do the job," writes Gordon. "I knew where such a tree was standing on one of our claims: an enormous spruce tree straight, tall and perfectly symmetrical. Jack and I felled it onto smaller skid trees so that it would slide into the water under its own momentum. The tree was 24 inches round at the base and 16 inches at the 100 foot mark. It was the perfect specimen of the type of spar Captain Cook noted from the bridge of his ship on his first trip into Nootka. He was looking for trees that would be suitable for masts for the British Navy."[135]

With business concluded at Ahousaht, Captain Gillam signals to the engine room to reverse engines. The *Maquinna* slowly backs out of Matilda Inlet, edging carefully toward wider waters. Al Bloom explains the tricky manoeuvres:

The inlet leading to Ahousaht was so narrow that the ship had to travel in reverse for half a mile or so on the way out, before there was enough room to turn around. I made the trip one night when it was so dark and foggy that I couldn't see either shore, but the *Maquinna* managed to be right on course and found that little dock, just by giving periodic blasts on the whistle and listening to the echoes. And then she retraced the route in reverse! The crews were fantastic seamen. Someone asked one of the captains how he could remember where all the rocks were and he replied, "I can't. I just know where they aren't."[136]

Once out of Matilda Inlet, the first part of the journey north up Millar Channel proves fairly straightforward until it narrows considerably at the north end, through the tight Hayden Passage between Flores and Obstruction Islands. Here the tide sometimes runs at 3 to

The *Princess Maquinna* approaching the Indian Chief
Copper Mine in Stewardson Inlet, Clayoquot Sound.
IMAGE COURTESY OF MIKE HAMILTON COLLECTION.

5 knots, depending which way the current flows, but once through,
Gillam changes course, heading west down Shelter Inlet and then
turning northwest into Sydney Inlet. The *Maquinna*'s destination is
up Stewardson Inlet, which branches westward about halfway up
Sydney Inlet. Once Captain Gillam turns the ship into Stewardson
Inlet he proceeds halfway up until he reaches the Indian Chief Copper Mine, Clayoquot Sound's most successful mining operation.

Mining—or the dream of mining—fired the imagination of countless prospectors in Clayoquot Sound, some of them arriving in the
area as early as the 1860s. Victoria newspapers referred to the sound
as "the mineral belt of the Island."[137] A number of gold rushes in
the area led to high hopes and bitter disappointment for many.
However, the Indian Chief Copper Mine in Stewardson Inlet led to
employment for many, and greatly increased cargo loads for the CPR
steamships. With the mine entrance halfway up the side of the inlet's

steep cliffs, an aerial tramway brought the ore down to a dock built on the shore, while a small sawmill kept itself busy cutting lumber for pit props and shoring. A concentrator, added during World War I when copper prices soared, helped the mine produce 300 tons of ore a day, all of which had to be transported by CPR steamers to Tacoma, Washington, for smelting.

As the *Maquinna*'s journey continues, the passengers, now familiar with the ship and its routine, fill in their time viewing the scenery, watching the loading and unloading of cargo and passengers, playing games on the upper deck—weather permitting—conversing with fellow travellers in the lounge, chatting to crew members, or napping in their cabins, all the while keeping an alert ear for the breakfast, lunch or dinner gong that calls them to the dining room for yet another superb CPR repast.

CHAPTER 12

HESQUIAHT AND ESTEVAN

FTER CLEARING Stewardson Inlet and the Indian Chief Copper Mine the *Princess Maquinna* steams back down Stewardson Inlet, then southeast and south down Sydney Inlet until she reaches open water beyond Sharp Point at the end of the Openit Peninsula. From there she heads north, and on her starboard side passes Refuge Cove, which boasts one of the area's most notable geological features, invisible from the ocean.

Every minute, the hot springs here produce 454 litres of water at a constant 52° C. These springs have been highly valued for centuries by the local Nuu-chah-nulth people, who called it *mok-she-kla-chuck* or "Smoking Water." In more recent times, passing boat crews and fishermen sometimes stopped to relax in the springs, where they would soak, wash the sweat and grime off their bodies, and clean their clothes. On this trip in 1924, however, the *Maquinna* steams past the cove without a second glance; with no one living there on a permanent basis, there's no need to stop. The place has changed immeasurably since 1924: now known more commonly as Hot Springs Cove, it has a well-established Indigenous village, a settler community, and has become one of the most popular tourist destinations on the coast.

Victoria-born Ivan Clarke saw the potential of Refuge Cove before other settlers. Clarke had been selling groceries and supplies from a converted fish packer on the west coast, and wanted a land base. In 1933 he pre-empted two large parcels of land in Refuge Cove, including the mile-long (2-km) trail to the hot springs. He established a store, becoming the first non-Indigenous resident of the cove. From the outset, he and his family relied heavily on connections to the *Maquinna*. In January 1935, with his store and a couple of habitable dwellings established, Clarke sent for his fiancée, Mabel, in Victoria. He made his way over to Ahousaht to meet her when she arrived aboard the *Maquinna,* and Rev. Joseph Jones of the Presbyterian Mission married the two aboard the ship. Captain William "Black" Thompson gave the bride away; Mary Livesley of Ahousaht and the *Maquinna*'s chief engineer Donald MacRaild acted as witnesses.[138] The newlyweds spent their honeymoon night aboard the *Maquinna*.

Clarke's enterprise grew to include a gas dock, a post office and eventually a fish-packing plant, prompting the *Maquinna* to begin making regular stops at Refuge Cove. Mabel became pregnant with her first of eight children, and when the time for the birth approached she would board the *Maquinna* and go to Victoria to have the baby. Ivan and his family travelled up and down the coast many times on "Old Faithful" and developed a great love for her. When the *Maquinna* retired from service in 1952, Ivan, who happened to be in Victoria at the time, attended the initial dismantling of the ship. He purchased all the ship's keys, including the stateroom keys, which are still in the possession of the Clarke family today. Later still, in 1955, Ivan and Mabel donated 14 of their original 48.5 hectare pre-emption to the provincial government for a park, suggesting the word "Maquinna" should be used in the park's name. The provincial government later acquired substantially more land surrounding the Clarkes' donated property, and the now 2,667-hectare park bears the name Maquinna Marine Provincial Park.

Ignoring the cove, the *Maquinna* steams northwest through open waters for Hesquiaht village, located on the southeast side of the Hesquiaht Peninsula, at the mouth of Purdon Creek and fronted by

The beach in front of the Hesquiaht village, date unknown. Note the variety of canoes. IMAGE COURTESY OF THE MOUNT ANGEL ABBEY LIBRARY.

a wide beach. This is the main village of the Hesquiaht First Nation and lies a short distance east of Estevan Point. In August 1774, four years before Captain James Cook arrived at Nootka, the Spanish vessel *Santiago* anchored off Estevan Point. Captain Juan Josef Pérez Hernández had been sent north from Mexico by his superiors to explore the northwest coast. When some of the Indigenous people saw the ship they hid themselves in fear, never having seen such a ship before, but a number of courageous warriors tentatively approached the vessel in their canoes. Pérez and his crew traded with them, obtaining sea otter skins and conical cedar hats in return for the knives, silver spoons, cloth and abalone shells the Spanish brought with them from California. This marked the first contact and trade between Europeans and Indigenous people on the west coast. Increasing winds put an end to the interaction, forcing Pérez to cut his anchor and sail south without landing, as he had planned to do, in order to claim sovereignty of the land for Spain. This omission would later prove costly for Spain when another European power, Britain, laid claim to the territory.

In 1869 Hesquiaht village and its people fell victim to one of the most appalling "tragedies of Victorian attitudes and relations between European and Aboriginal peoples."[139] In February of that year, the sailing barque *John Bright* foundered on the rocks off Hesquiaht Peninsula near Estevan Point in a vicious winter storm. Eleven people were on board, including the captain's wife and children. No one survived. Enormous waves pounded the ship to pieces, and the bodies of the crew and passengers became horribly mutilated by the constant battering of the surf and rocks. News of the tragedy did not reach Victoria until early March, when sealing captain James Christensen arrived relating a sensational story to local newspapers. He reported seeing local Hesquiaht wearing victims' clothing and jewellery, prompting the newspapers to speculate that the victims had "all undeniably found a watery grave, or have fallen by the hands of the West Coast savages." The stories continued to speculate on what might have happened: that the captain had been shot while running away from "the cruel savages"; that "prisoners had been thrown down and their heads removed while they piteously begged for mercy" and that the children's nursemaid, Beatrice Holden, had been "delivered up to the young men of the tribe, dragged into the bush where her cries filled the air for hours."[140]

Eventually, in May 1870, Governor Frederick Seymour sent the steam-driven warship HMS *Sparrowhawk* north from Victoria to investigate. After examining the remains of the exhumed bodies of the *John Bright*, the *Sparrowhawk*'s surgeon attested he could find no medical evidence indicating that the bodies had been decapitated by human hands, and that the gnawing of animals and the pounding of the bodies in the surf and on the rocks accounted for their mutilated condition.

Nevertheless, after the Hesquiaht chiefs refused to turn over the men who stood accused of these crimes, the Royal Marines set fire to the village houses and the ship's cannons destroyed the canoes on the beach. The captain then ordered seven Hesquiaht men seized and taken to Victoria to be tried.

Following two separate trials, each deeply flawed, with a questionable interpreter, and each reported in hysterical language by the Victoria newspapers, an all-white jury of twenty men found two of the accused, Katkinna and John Anietsachist, guilty of murder. The judge sentenced them to be hanged. Taken back to Hesquiaht in chains aboard the *Sparrowhawk*, the two condemned men, along with their Hesquiaht brethren, stood by as carpenters erected a gallows on the beach. With the whole Hesquiaht tribe forced to watch, the two were hanged, as cannons boomed out over the harbour.

In 1875, eleven years after this tragedy, the Belgian Roman Catholic missionary Father Augustin Brabant arrived at the village, determined Hesquiaht would be the centre of his west coast mission. Here he erected the first church in Clayoquot Sound, St. Antonine, an imposing wooden structure that later burned down, to be rebuilt in 1891.

Brabant would live among the Hesquiaht for thirty-seven years, remaining there until ill health forced him to leave in 1912. He oversaw the construction of Catholic churches in several locations on the west coast, and was responsible for raising funds to start Christie School, at Kakawis. During Brabant's first year at Hesquiaht, he survived an attack by one of the chiefs, nearly dying of his injuries, but he never faltered in his determination to convert the people he thought of as "his Indians." Tall and powerfully built, Brabant brooked no opposition, establishing himself as a towering force to be reckoned with, up and down the west coast.

Shortly after Brabant died, a very different, but equally memorable, character entered the scene at Hesquiaht Harbour. In 1915 the indomitable Ada Annie Rae-Arthur disembarked from the *Princess Maquinna* into a waiting canoe at Hesquiaht village. With her, her husband Willie Rae-Arthur, their three children and little else barring the determination to homestead in the area on a pre-empted tract of land some 6 miles (almost 10 km) inside the harbour. Over time she established a highly productive garden there, at the eastern end of the harbour in Boat Basin. Later dubbed "Cougar Annie" because of her prowess in killing cougars, Ada Annie raised eight children, operated a general store and post office, and ran a mail-order nursery business. From the five-acre garden she created in the wilderness, she mailed plants and bulbs to customers as far away as Winnipeg. Her children and her first husband Willie would row the 6 miles (nearly 10 km) across to Hesquiaht to deliver her packages for shipment on the *Princess Maquinna* and collect supplies. On one of these journeys Willie drowned, on July 14, 1936. Later, one of her children, Laurie, also drowned in the harbour. Cougar Annie remained at Boat Basin for some seventy years, outlasting a total of four husbands. She died in 1987 at the age of 97.

On this trip up the coast it is clear that because of the exposed beach fronting the village, landing and loading goods at Hesquiaht always means a "boat landing" for the *Maquinna*. Canoes come out from the village and supplies are unloaded from the side doors of the steamer, while passengers struggle down the rope ladder extended to the vessels below. Off-loading cows for the mission can be particularly tricky. "Shorty" Wright would winch the unhappy creatures up in a sling and lower them into the water, and they would swim to the beach. If there were calves, crewmen would tie their feet and then ease them into the canoes to be carried ashore. In short order, about fifteen minutes after arriving here, the cargo doors close, the ship's whistle sounds and the *Maquinna* sets off once again.

As the *Maquinna* rounds Hesquiaht Peninsula, her passengers can see the distinctive Estevan Point Lighthouse, set in a small bay called the Hole-in-the-Wall. Building began in 1908 and ended in 1910. At 98 ft (30 m) tall it is one of the largest free-standing concrete structures on the west coast, featuring eight flying buttresses anchoring it to the rocks against the blasts of storms and tremors of earthquakes. Early in World War II it would gain national and international attention, having apparently been shelled by a Japanese submarine.

Prior to launching its surprise attack on US forces at Pearl Harbor, Hawaii, on December 7, 1941, the Japanese navy sent six submarines

Estevan Point Lighthouse, built 1908–10. In 1941 a Japanese submarine reportedly fired shells at Estevan, causing panic in Canada and leading to increased wartime defences along the west coast.
IMAGE C-05328 COURTESY OF THE ROYAL BC MUSEUM.

across the Pacific to attack shipping and shore installations on the coast of North America, aiming to create panic and fear among the citizens of the West Coast. One attacked a ship off California, killing five crew members, and later fired shells from its deck gun at an oil complex near Santa Barbara. The following summer, on June 20, 1942, Estevan Point Lighthouse received twenty-five incoming 5.5-inch shells purportedly fired by a Japanese submarine. Pandemonium erupted at the light station and among the Hesquiaht villagers. More recently there has been some skepticism about whether a Japanese submarine did indeed fire the shells, but the Japanese captain, who survived the war, admitted to the attack, and when questioned, survivors of a Japanese submarine that was sunk a year after the incident, in New Zealand, "admitted that they were responsible for the attack."[141]

Skeptics believe the shelling was a false-flag operation from Allied sources attempting to convince the Canadian public of the danger facing its virtually undefended coast, and hoping to counter the reluctance of anti-conscription Quebecers to become involved in the war. Whatever the cause, the shelling of Estevan Point Lighthouse certainly caused panic, fuelling the controversial decision by the Canadian government to intern all of the 23,000 Japanese living in Canada, mostly along Canada's west coast.

In 1924 all of this turmoil lies in the future, as the *Maquinna* heads across open waters for Yuquot, or Friendly Cove. Here the Good Ship enters the territory of the people from whom she derived her name—Princess Maquinna being the daughter of the most famous and powerful chief on the west coast, Chief Maquinna of the Mowachaht people.

CHAPTER 13

NOOTKA SOUND

S THE *Princess Maquinna* steams toward Yuquot she crosses the mouth of Nootka Sound. For passengers who know their British Columbia history, these are highly significant waters, for on March 29, 1778, momentous events took place here.

After sailing across the Pacific Ocean from Hawaii, while on his third circumnavigation of the globe on a mission to find the Northwest Passage, the British naval captain James Cook sailed into Nootka Sound. He sought shelter to repair his two storm-battered ships, HMS *Resolution* and HMS *Discovery*. Having been greeted by some of the Mowachaht men in canoes, who thought the newcomers "were the dead returning ... in floating houses,"[142] Cook sailed past the village of Yuquot, anchoring in a small cove sheltered by an island. He named these landmarks Resolution Cove, after his ship, and Bligh Island, for one of his midshipmen, William Bligh, later the infamous master of HMS *Bounty*.

Cook and his men stayed in Nootka Sound for over a month making repairs, cutting new masts and spars, brewing spruce beer and trading with the local Mowachaht people and their mighty chief Maquinna. As the most powerful chief on the west coast, he could muster an army of 300-400 warriors when needed, and presided over an estimated 1,000 people at Yuquot, the tribe's main summer residence. Other tribal members lived in various other summer encampments. In winter Maquinna and his people lived in Tahsis and in other smaller villages well inside Nootka Sound, away from winter storms on the outer coast. In spring the Mowachaht moved back to Yuquot to be nearer the ocean, where they would hunt whales, northern fur seals and sea otters in the summer months. The Indigenous people particularly prized items they could not produce themselves: industrially manufactured, mostly metal, items such as knives, chisels, nails, needles and buttons. Cook's men traded a large quantity of such items for a total of three hundred sea otter pelts, initially using these soft furs as mattresses in their hammocks. Much later on their journey, when they arrived in Canton, where such furs were very rare and highly valued, they traded them at a profit and bought porcelain, silks and spices, which in turn they later sold in England for a huge profit over the cost of the original knives and chisels. Their returns, in some cases twice the annual pay of a seaman, precipitated the sea otter fur trade that would bring avid traders from many nations to Nootka Sound and to the entire northwest coast of North America.

Yuquot, on Nootka Island, can rightly claim to be one of the most beautiful and intriguing locations on the west coast. As the *Princess Maquinna* rounds the Nootka Lighthouse on Hog Island (now San Rafael Island) and enters the cove, passengers pass the site of Fort San Miguel, built on San Miguel Island by the Spanish. In 1789, Spanish naval ships arrived from Mexico, more than a decade after Cook's visit, and occupied the island in an attempt to lay claim to the area, which Cook had already claimed for Britain. This incursion precipitated a diplomatic squabble that brought Britain and Spain to the brink of war. The Nootka Convention of 1790 brought an end to the wrangle, which eventually saw Spain pay restitution to Britain for ships she had damaged, and relinquishing all claims to the west coast of North America.

Once inside the cove, visitors see ahead of them a long curving beach above which "is a row of Indian houses, about 100 yards above the shore line," as Inspector Brodie writes in his 1918 report. "In front of the village they have two of the finest totem poles on the

Yuquot, or Friendly Cove, on Nootka Island is a pivotal location in West Coast history. Britain and Spain nearly went to war because of a confrontation here that ended with the signing of the Nootka Convention in 1790.
IMAGE I-55452 COURTESY OF THE ROYAL BC MUSEUM.

Pacific Coast. One is crowned by a figure of Capt. Vancouver in a grotesquely painted black silk hat. They have a large assembly hall [a longhouse] in which they hold festivals, etc . . . To the right of the village there is a small clearing where a little church is situated."[143] In 1889 Father Brabant built the church Brodie refers to.

Brodie's expansive report continues, pointing out that the first European ship ever built in British Columbia was built here at Yuquot. Captain John Meares arrived at Nootka in 1788, bringing with him twenty-nine Chinese workers, and set them to work building the 45-ton *North West America* in a small cove inside Yuquot. Once launched, he employed it trading for sea otter pelts up and down the coast.

What caught Brodie's attention in particular was the graveyard, to him "one of the most interesting places on the Pacific Coast." Used by the Mowachaht people, the individual burial plots all had individual fences:

There are numbers of small houses built over the various graves. One house in particular is very amusing. After completing the house and shingling it all, including the roof, two window frames with four panes of glass in each one, are carefully nailed on top of the shingles on the room, two on each side, so as to give the necessary light within. One grave is of particular interest. The plot is of a fair size with a good fence around it. A monument in the centre informs you that this is the son of Chief Napoleon Maquinna. It is customary for the Indians to make sacrifices for the dead, so the Chief has placed on each side of the grave two very fine dugouts. At the back of the grave in the centre of the fence, is a small model of a ship which the boy once played with, and on each side are the ends of an iron bedstead, with some wash basins and some other trinkets. On another grave of an Indian woman is a sewing machine, wash basins and baskets, together with several other small effects. One man who died has over his grave a bicycle pump, a lantern, and old gas tank, lunch basket and some wash basins. Another has a gramaphone [*sic*]. Sewing machines and bedsteads seem to be quite popular. One little child's grave has a go-cart on top of it. Altogether the graveyard is rather pathetic, and I am afraid if many tourists visited it they would steal some of the baskets and other articles as souvenirs, although it would cause a great row among the Indians.[144]

On August 12, 1924, the *Princess Maquinna* arrived at Yuquot with then Lieutenant Governor Walter Nichol, Dr. C.F. Newcombe of the Provincial Museum and Judge F.W. Howay of the Historic Sites and Monument Board of Canada, as well as other dignitaries and onlookers. The lieutenant governor unveiled an 11-ft (3.3-m) cairn commemorating Cook's "discovery" of Nootka Sound. Tofino author Dorothy Abraham wrote of the event in her book *Lone Cone*: "When we arrived at Nootka, Indians in their war canoes came out and encircled the ship [the *Princess Maquinna*]. They looked quite frightening in all their war paint, fish blood etc. The cairn to Captain

The *Maquinna* pulling away from the dock at the Nootka Cannery, situated a few kilometres east of Yuquot, in 1918. H.W. BRODIE PHOTO, COURTESY OF WALLY CHUNG COLLECTION, SPECIAL COLLECTIONS UBC.

Cook was unveiled with an impressive ceremony, and one tried to visualize Nootka as it had been in his day. Later the Indians, adorned in their weird and grotesque garments sprinkled with duck down and wearing alarming head pieces, put on some excellent Potlatch dances."[145] Gillam's friend Father Charles Moser acted as interpreter for Nichol and Nootka chief Napoleon Maquinna, descendant of the original Chief Maquinna. "The officials of the CPR company allowed the steamer to remain at Nootka Sound for an extra half-day in order that ample time might be provided for the ceremony."[146]

After stopping at Yuquot on our imagined 1924 trip, the *Maquinna* sets off again for a run of 1.75 nautical miles (3.2 km) to the Nootka Cannery, opened in 1917 and situated in Boca del Infierno Bay farther into the Sound. There she picks up cases of salmon and pilchard products.

Beginning in the 1930s, the *Maquinna* would leave Nootka Cannery and, instead of going back out into the Pacific, would head deeper into the sound toward Tahsis, where the Gibson brothers were then engaged in logging. If we take a diversion here, a few years ahead of our current journey, we can revisit that era when logging thrived on the fringes of these inlets, where small independent hand loggers, or "gyppo loggers," operated from float camps.

"The word 'gyppo' has been used in many ways to describe many things about our logging industry," writes Bill Moore. "It generally is used to describe a logger who is, among other things, 'a loner,' an innovator who can patch things up and make them 'run,' an 'owner of a very small camp' or a 'maverick.' To operate a camp in a gyppo way could mean to operate on the cheap, to use haywire equipment or to simply operate with a small crew."[147]

Al Bloom describes his journey up Tahsis Inlet on the *Maquinna* in 1937 when he witnessed these gyppo outfits, hand-logging the side hills in the days before logging trucks and chainsaws.

The slopes were covered with trees—fir, hemlock, cedar—and a lot of scrub bush, right down to the high water mark. I soon saw my first small, gyppo logging show (it was anything but small to me) where everything was on big log floats, jill-poked [secured] from shore by long logs, and anchored in place with cables running ashore and tied to big stumps. The cookhouse and bunkhouse were on floats, and on another float there was an A-frame, made of two heavy poles about one hundred feet high, lashed together at the top and held upright by several cables. At the bottom of the A-frame was the donkey engine, powered at first by a steam boiler, but later by the more efficient diesel engine, and connected to a three-drum winch. One drum held the straw-line, the second the heavier haul-back line, and the third the heavy mainline.[148]

The three cables that ran from the three drums on the float were essential for dragging the cut logs down the mountain slopes to the booming ground in the water below.

A typical gyppo logging operation, or "show." The A-frame erected on a float camp dragged logs down from side hills to the booming ground, in the foreground. IMAGE NA-11181_141(A) COURTESY OF THE ROYAL BC MUSEUM.

The A frame shows were tough to work on; you had to be a mountain climber in heavy caulk boots, able to scramble over and under
logs, pulling and pushing heavy chokers into position, and getting
out of the way before the whistle punk started a load on its way
down hill. As the *Maquinna* moved through the quiet waters, we
passed a couple of these floating rigs, and could see many places
where they had been working, taking the easy-to-get logs along
the shore. The sides of the mountains were stripped clean of all
greenery as far as the mainline cable could reach—usually a few
thousand feet—but the hills and valleys away from the water were
left for a different breed of logger to come later with his mechanical
equipment on caterpillar tracks.[149]

When Al Bloom made this trip on the *Maquinna*, in 1937, the
Gibson brothers from Ahousaht had branched out and were now running a large logging operation near Tahsis, at the head of Tahsis Inlet.

This camp was all on big floats, one of the *Maquinna*'s regular stops. There was Gordon Gibson standing on the float, a big
cigar clamped in the corner of his mouth, but it didn't stop him
from roaring a greeting to the captain on the bridge. He was big,
burly, loud, the typical bull-of-the-woods if there ever was one, in
his bone-dry clothes with the pants stagged [cut] halfway up his
legs, and his jacket wide open showing the bright, wide braces
that he used to hold his pants up. His feet were shoved into high-
top caulk boots with the tops wide open and the laces flying in the
breeze, so he could kick them off in a hurry whenever he entered
a camp building... When the *Maquinna* docked he would go
on board, carrying his caulk boots in his hand, and head down-
stairs to the lounge, where he put his stocking feet up on a coffee
table in a most relaxed manner and enjoyed an hour's conversation with the people around him. The oldest brother, Clarke,
took care of the Vancouver office. They couldn't lose, with Gordon to ramrod and bulldoze his way through any job around the

woods or on the boats, and the others [his older brothers Clarke, Jack and Earson] to smooth over the rough edges he left along the way.[150]

Later still, in 1945, the Gibson brothers would build a huge sawmill in Tahsis, bringing great prosperity to the small village and providing the *Maquinna* with even more business. Finished with Tahsis, the *Maquinna* heads back down the inlet before turning up Tahsis Narrows, which connects Tahsis and Esperanza Inlets and separates Nootka Island from Vancouver Island itself. Just after turning into the narrows and running across Blowhole Bay, the ship reaches the Ceepeecee pilchard cannery, built in 1926. One of the most curious names on the west coast, the cannery derived its name from the initials of its first owner, the Canadian Packing Company. In 1934 Richie and Norman Nelson bought the plant and hired Dal Lutes to manage it. Al Bloom wrote:

The Nelson brothers seldom came to Ceepeecee, as it was a two-week round trip on the *Maquinna*, but let their manager run the plant. Lutes was a character in his own right with a voice and vocabulary that would do justice to a mule skinner, a job that he handled in his younger years when he freighted from Steveston to Vancouver over a wagon road now known as Granville Street. He ran Ceepeecee as if he owned it, and when the only contact with head office was a shortwave radio, it is small wonder that this should be so. To all and sundry, Lutes was Mr. Ceepeecee, loved and respected by many, hated by others. When the *Maquinna* docked, the tourists would flock ashore to stretch their legs. To reach the local store they had to follow a ten-foot-wide plank walkway between the cannery and the reduction plant, plowing their way through various strong smells produced by the reduction plant and by rotting offal on the beach. They covered their noses with perfumed handkerchiefs and rushed through this section, hoping to reach fresh air again.[151]

Loading cases of pilchard into the hold of the
Princess Maquinna at Ceepeecee in the 1930s.
IMAGE I-26234 COURTESY OF THE ROYAL BC MUSEUM.

A ten-minute boat journey northwest of Ceepeecee lies the Esperanza Mission Hospital, established in 1937 by Dr. Herman McLean and the Nootka Mission Association, an offshoot of the Shantymen's Christian Association. The *Maquinna* does not make regular stops at the hospital itself, but drops off the mission's mail and supplies at Ceepeecee where the mission's own boats—used for medical and missionary work—pick them up.

Underway again, and still on our time-travel to the 1930s, the *Maquinna* steams out of Hecate Channel and into Zeballos Inlet where she turns northeast toward the gold-mining town of Zeballos at the head of the inlet. Prospectors would find gold here in 1936, setting off a spectacular gold rush in the midst of the Great Depression in one of the wettest places on the west coast.

CHAPTER 14

ZEBALLOS AND ESPERANZA

I N 1791, Captain Alejandro Malaspina of the Spanish navy sailed to the northern end of what would become Zeballos Inlet. He named it in honour of a lieutenant on his ship, Ciriaco Cevallos. Few outsiders visited the area until 1924, when some prospectors found significant traces of gold there and registered the Eldorado claim.

During the economic downturn of the 1930s other desperate gold seekers came to the area. "A new breed of prospectors arrived on the scene," writes Walter Guppy, the Tofino author and authority on early mining on the west coast. "These were the fugitives from the hopelessness of the soup kitchens and relief camps... Some were fishermen who had gone broke when the markets for fish collapsed... In 1936 one of these bushwhackers, named Alfred Bird, found a vein that gave spectacular assays in gold."[152]

Once the word got out, hundreds of hopeful gold seekers arrived and a small village quickly grew: this became Zeballos. "In 1936 the *Maquinna* began to make it a regular stop on its coastal journey. It would be loaded stem to stern with freight, and besides the regular west coast passengers, she would carry another load of men and women mad for gold. Prominent engineers from all over the world, promoters, prospectors, clerks, men from every walk of life journeyed to Zeballos," writes an author with the *nom de plume* "Old

Main Street of the gold-mining town of Zeballos in the 1940s.

Timer" in a *West Coast Advocate* article from 1955. "Nearly every cabin [on the *Maquinna*] has its quota of liquor, and sometimes more. There was a continual whoop de do from the time the schooner left Victoria until she reached Zeballos, where there was neither wharf nor road."[153]

Old Timer goes on to describe how the *Maquinna* anchored off-shore, and how all freight had to be carried ashore in small boats, while passengers often piggy-backed over the tidal flats to dry land.

Among the thirty or so active claims being worked near Zeballos, the one named Privateer developed into the chief mine, producing about half of the gold that came out of the area. The little village thrived, becoming a bustling community of 1,500 people and boasting four beer parlours, a liquor store and a bawdy house. Its main wooden-planked street sported false-fronted buildings like a town in a Western movie.

In 1937 Hugh Skinner served as the freight manager in Zeballos and also owned the local store with partners Gene Llewellyn and Roy Seton. Two decades later Skinner recounted in a *Daily Colonist* article the heart-warming events of Christmas Eve that year. He tells how the west coast had been experiencing severe gales, which local mariners were calling "the worst in living memory." The storms and an accident prevented the *Maquinna* from calling at Zeballos for ten days because she had suffered "buckled plates caused in a slight brush with a rock and had to be towed to Victoria for repairs."[154]

During those ten days the small town almost entirely ran out of essential supplies, and the small hospital ran dangerously low on medicine; one patient died for lack of a sulpha drug and others, including two small children, were in dire straits. "It looked like the bleakest kind of holiday for all concerned and especially of the some 40 or 50 children who had looked forward with great anticipation to the concert and party that had been planned for months,"[155] writes Skinner.

Food, medicine, gasoline, kerosene and booze—everything the town required—depended on the arrival of the *Maquinna*, and everyone in the village waited in anticipation. The hours dragged by as people kept looking down the inlet for the supply ship scheduled to arrive at noon, and now long overdue. "Then suddenly it came, the full throated roar of the *Maquinna*'s great steam whistle... We rushed to the window, threw our arms round one another and danced a jig. My God what a beautiful sight! There she was just sifting between Twin Islets, dead slow and getting ready to drop anchor, after which the tarps would come off the hatches and she would be ready to disgorge her precious cargo."[156]

Skinner and his partners threw on their coats, mufflers, toques and rubber wear and towed their barge through the wind and sleet to the side of the *Maquinna*.

"Okay Captain," I shouted. "Let's have the medical supplies and the booze first and we'll take those ashore in the power skiff, then we'll load the rest onto the scow." The scene in the bay had an aura of unreality. Floodlights piercing the slanting rain, the hissing steam winches groaning as they deposited load after load on the deck of the huge scow. There were sides of beef, crates of turkeys, fresh vegetables, mountain of assorted canned goods, flour, bacon, drums of gasoline and kerosene. It was now 4:30 p.m. and the children's Christmas concert was set for eight o'clock and we were only half loaded, however, by six it was all loaded and what a beautiful sight it was. Great mounds of goodies with tantalizing labels on boxes, over there, Ocean Spray cranberry sauce, and look there, Crosse and Blackwell plum pudding were the ones that seemed to jump at me as I steered my precious cargo to the shore.[157]

When the scow slid onto the clamshell beach Skinner realized he faced a problem—there was no one to help him unload, since most of the town's menfolk had already hit the local bars, and were joyfully tucking into the stock of Christmas booze that had arrived earlier. So he went into the bars where "whiskey flowed like water and loud conversation and raucous singing were the order of the day."

Calling for quiet he announced: "You all know there are 200 tons of supplies for you out there on my scow and you are not going to get it this night unless you and me make a deal. You all know that in one hour's time the Christmas Party for the children starts at the school. Well, here's the deal, you help me get the presents and food to the kid's party, and help get the supplies to the store and maybe we can then all share Christmas in a meaningful way."[158]

Soon forty or fifty half-drunken men lurched out of the bars and began unloading the scow onto a couple of trucks so that by eight o'clock the vehicles bearing the toys, food, crackerjacks and Japanese oranges were chugging up to the school. The men carried box after box into the classroom where parents, children and teacher welcomed them. "Merriment reigned supreme as children screamed with unbridled joy as each man deposited his burden on the makeshift stage. 'Merry Christmas' they shouted and the air was full of good will and warm feelings."[159]

The men then headed back out into the storm and rain to carry load after load of goods to the store, which then opened for business at midnight and would not shut until 4 a.m.

Sides of beef were attacked with gusto. Gene was hacking one up with a double bitted axe as he shouted: "Its four bits [50 cents] a pound no matter whether it comes off the head or the tail." Crates of turkeys were opened and emptied. The women found several bolts of cloth and were busy pawing and clucking over their find as many had not seen any of this for months. Everywhere business was brisk, shoes, shirts, trousers, socks, lamps, hardware, cases of fruit. The fresh vegetables were gone in an instant. There was an unrestrained orgy of buying and this happening at 2 a.m. Christmas morning. People were leaving with carts, wheelbarrows, back packs, all loaded with sustenance. All through the buying spree there prevailed an air of good fellowship and the night was not marred by a single untoward incident. Later, as I was blissfully slipping off to dreamland I swear I heard a voice say from on high: "A Merry Christmas to all and to all a good night," and the wind howled and all the town slept in peace.[160]

When Edward Gillam captained the *Maquinna*, throughout the 1910s and 1920s, every year he enacted the part of Santa Claus for children in remote coastal communities, cramming the wheelhouse and even his own sleeping quarters with parcels, to the point that he had nowhere to lie down at night.

In the decade or so the Zeballos mines were in operation, gold worth about $10 million (in contemporary values) left Zeballos on the *Princess Maquinna*—today, the same gold would be worth some $575 million. The story goes that occasionally the Zeballos postmaster slept with a rifle under his pillow because of the $100,000 in gold bricks he had under his bed as he waited for "Old Faithful" to arrive. The *Maquinna* carried the gold bars to Victoria, from where they would eventually be shipped to the Royal Canadian Mint in Ottawa.

With business completed in Zeballos, the *Maquinna* would head back down Zeballos Inlet and then turn west, travelling 14 nautical miles (26 km) down Esperanza Inlet and back into the open Pacific, where she would head north for 15.5 nautical miles (29 km), aiming for Kyuquot Sound on what could be one of the roughest legs of her journey. On our imagined trip in 1924, the ship would not have visited Zeballos at all—the rousing adventures of that community lay at least a decade in the future. But no matter what the time period, the open seas at the end of Esperanza Inlet remain the same.

One of the reasons for this stretch of coast between Esperanza Inlet and Kyuquot Sound being so difficult, says David Young, former captain of the MV *Uchuck III*, who ran this route regularly in the 1980s and 1990s, is:

> The near shore route that we followed between the Sounds is only ten to twelve fathoms [60–72 ft/18–22 m] deep, making storm seas shorter and steeper, more than is the case far out to sea. On one trip it took me five hours to go from Kyuquot to Esperanza Inlet, normally a one-hour run. We had started out in a rising gale that gave us a royal beating even after we moved ten [nautical] miles [18.5 km] offshore to try and find easier traveling. Apart from the wild ride, the difficult bit was turning to enter Esperanza Inlet, which left us beam-on to the wind and sea and our helmsman was barely able to control our direction of travel. Even with full power applied he had to keep the helm nearly hard-to-port to steer the course that was needed.[161]

Given the fair weather on our summer trip in 1924, the *Maquinna* requires a mere hour of steaming before she rounds Rugged Point at the entrance to Kyuquot Sound, and cruises past Union and Whiteley Islands on her port side. She then steers south into Cachalot Inlet, where the stench forewarns passengers that they are arriving at the Cachalot whaling station. Established in 1907 by Captains Sprott Balcon and William Grant, the plant and its whalers caught and processed an average of four hundred whales a year, shipping the oil to Proctor and Gamble in Cincinnati, Ohio, to make soap. The bones were ground and shipped to California to become fertilizer. During World War I the plant canned 60,000 cases of whale meat for human consumption; reportedly it tasted like salty beef. Inspector W.H. Brodie describes Cachalot whaling station as he saw it on his trip on the *Maquinna* in 1918:

> The population of the whaling station consists of about 20 whites and 30 or more Indians. It is operated by the Victoria Whaling Co. They are canning the whale meat this year, and have a capacity of 2000 cases a day... Unfortunately, there were no whales at the station, but they were busy cutting up some of the heads, and the canning industry was working at full speed, as was the rendering plant and the fertilizer plant. Everything in connection with the whale is utilized. There is no waste. Two of the steel whaling boats were in the harbour and two others were at sea. They catch the whales between 30 and 40 miles [50 to 65 km] from the station. When caught they are immediately blown up with air, and when a sufficient number are taken are towed to the station. They have had as many as 13 at the station in a single day... Mr. Ruck, the General Manager, travelled North with us, and gave us some interesting information in regard to the station. He also presented us with some very fine whales' teeth and some whales' ear drums. They obtain about $2,000.00 worth of revenue from each whale, and have made as high as $5,000.00 from a sperm whale. From a sperm whale they have got as high as 80 barrels of oil. They generally extract as much as 35 to 40 barrels of oil from the ordinary whales. We cast off at 4:40 PM, and had a splendid trip, with fairly good sun, through the small islands to Kyuquot Village.[162]

In the 1940s and 1950s, before heading back out into the Pacific again, the *Maquinna* would sail north across Kyuquot Sound to Chamiss Bay, where the Gibson brothers ran a logging camp. Such a trip is not on the agenda in 1924, perhaps just as well, for it is unlikely Captain Gillam could go anywhere near Chamiss Bay without being assailed by rueful memories, which go back to the days when he skippered the SS *Tees,* before he became master of the *Maquinna.*

Cachalot whaling station in Kyuquot Sound with a
whale awaiting processing on the slip, circa 1920s.
IMAGE A-08855 COURTESY OF THE ROYAL BC MUSEUM.

On Sunday November 26, 1911, while captaining the SS *Tees,* Gillam was making his way down from Holberg, at the north end of the Island, to Victoria. When he reached Kyuquot Sound he turned eastward to make a call in Easy Inlet, on the north side of the sound about 10 nautical miles (18.5 km) from its entrance. There he picked up 150 tons of pottery clay at the Easy Creek pits. When backing away from the dock, however, the *Tees* struck a submerged rock, stripping off her propeller and damaging her rudder. Gillam immediately anchored the ship, ordering his radio operator to begin sending out SOS messages. Because of the *Tees*'s location amid the sheer rocky walls of the inlet and surrounding mountains, no one heard or acknowledged his signals. This meant that the ship, its twenty-one-man crew and its thirty-eight passengers were, to all intents and purposes, isolated and lost. Not hearing any regular radio messages from the ship, speculation soon arose in Victoria that the vessel had sunk.

Gillam, fearing that his repeated radio messages had not been received, sent one of the ship's open boats to row to Estevan Point Lighthouse, some 55 nautical miles (100 km) to the south. The lighthouse possessed the only radio transmitter in the area, and it would be able to send a message of the mishap to CPR headquarters in Victoria. Increasingly bad weather, however, forced the lifeboat crew to return to the ship after two horrendous days fighting the elements. "With seas lifting over us, drenched, hungry and cold, we ran in under Rugged Point, and found an abandoned Indian shack, and camped there."[163]

Those remaining on the *Tees* settled in for the long haul. Chief Steward Aspdin takes up the story:

When we anchored in Easy Creek I lost no time arranging to make the passengers comfortable. We fortunately had some good musical talent, so we arranged concerts, mock trials, etc, and spent as comfortable a time as possible under the circumstances. One had a piccolo and with his solos, some songs and other entertainment, we passed the time ... It was decided to make the provisions spin out by serving only two meals/day. On the 3rd day a ship's boat rowed to Kyuquot village where a bullock was slaughtered and the meat brought back in the boat.[164]

Unknown to Gillam and the people on the *Tees*, one of their radio messages had been picked up, and rescue vessels set off from various parts of the coast, in a howling winter gale, for Kyuquot Sound to search for the ship.

Eventually, on Saturday morning, December 2, rescue vessels reached the *Tees*, and were relieved to find all well. The *Daily Colonist* wrote:

The complement on board suffered nothing more than the missing of one meal of the usual three, and they sang and laughed, and enjoyed the amusements the ship's officers provided for them, while thousands imagined pictures that differed immensely from this condition of affairs. Many saw a wrecked ship, her decks awash with breaking seas, death and disaster, and for fear that the seas might be battering the steel sides of the staunch coaster.[165]

Ironically, in February 1919 the *Princess Maquinna*, with Captain Gilliam again in charge, also lost its propeller in the same Easy Inlet and had to be towed to Victoria. Doubly ironic is the fact that when the Pacific Salvage Company received the contract to go and find the *Maquinna*'s missing propeller, in March 1919, it chartered the *Tees*, which by then had been retired from regular service, to do the search. But after four days of putting divers down they failed to find the propeller in the 150-ft (45-m) depth.[166]

Because the entrance to Walters Cove, which holds Kyuquot village, is too narrow for the *Maquinna* to enter, she off-loads passengers and freight at Chamiss Bay, and smaller boats carry passengers and freight the 6.5 nautical miles (12 km) southwest to Kyuquot. As the *Maquinna* makes her way out of Kyuquot Sound, she passes the entrance to Walters Cove. Well protected from the wild Pacific storms that often rage just outside its narrow entrance, the cove is one of the safest harbours on the coast and includes a general store and a number of houses connected by a boardwalk. The east side of the cove houses a Kyuquot First Nation village. For many years fishermen in their boats sought the shelter of Walters Cove during storms, and it became locally know as "Bullshit Cove" because of the tall tales told by those fishermen while they waited out storms.

Once past Walters Island, the ship heads out into the open waters of the Pacific, heading north around the Brooks Peninsula, with Cape Cook at its northwest point, and into Quatsino Sound. Here, the *Maquinna* will make her final stops on the northern leg of her ten-day run.

CHAPTER 15

QUATSINO SOUND

ROOKS PENINSULA sticks out the side of Vancouver Island's west coast like a large fist. If passengers have avoided sea-sickness so far, they'll certainly be challenged here. Should they still be upright, they will see one of the finest sights of the entire voyage, Solander Island, named after the naturalist aboard Captain Cook's first voyage. Standing just under a mile (1.5 km) off the coast it rises high out of the sea and resembles Cathedral Peak in the Canadian Rockies, with heavy seas breaking over the rocks in clouds of spray. On two of its sloping sides, hundreds of sea lions lounge, barking and belching, as well as thousands of screeching seabirds, creating a cacophony of sound. When Captain Gillam sounds the ship's whistle, the sea lions flop down the sides of the rocks and into the sea, making a great hubbub.

Once the *Maquinna* rounds Cape Cook, at the northwestern tip of Brooks Peninsula, and crosses Brooks Bay, Captain Gillam and his helmsman keep an eye out for the Kains Island Lighthouse at the western entrance of Forward Inlet, branching north from Quatsino Sound. At night, the light helps guide vessels into Winter Harbour, the next port of call. Built with great difficulty in 1908, the Kains Island Lighthouse, 5.5 nautical miles (10 km) out from Winter Har-bour, represents one of the loneliest postings for any lightkeeper on the west coast. In 1918 the *Daily Colonist* reported the effort of James Sadler, the lightkeeper, to help his wife Catherine, who "has

A container of clams from the Leesons' cannery. BEN LEESON PHOTO,
IMAGE VPL 71638 COURTESY OF THE VANCOUVER PUBLIC LIBRARY.

become violently insane from the awful loneliness of the west coast
and two of her four children were in a precarious state through lack
of food. Sadler was found at his post ... after he had exhausted himself in his efforts to keep his wife from committing suicide."[167]

Once past the light, the *Maquinna* steams north into Forward
Inlet and into Winter Harbour, so named because it provided a safe
haven for sailing vessels during winter storms. It is the most westerly
settlement on Vancouver Island. Kwakiutl villagers and a few fishermen and loggers live here. Jobe (Joseph) Leeson, originally from
Coventry, England, arrived here in 1894 with his family, and he
established a trading post, J.L. Leeson & Sons Trading, serving the
local Kwakiutl people and visiting whaling and sealing ships. In 1904
Leeson established the Winter Harbour Canning Company, canning
clams and crabs and employing up to forty Chinese and First Nations

workers. Credited with inventing condensed clams, he and his sons also sold salted fish, and made wooden barrels.

Early in his life, Leeson's son Ben acquired an interest in photography, and over the years took hundreds of photographs of life in Winter Harbour and the Quatsino Sound area, with a special interest in the "flat-heads" of the Kwakiutl women. Local custom dictated that the heads of little girls be bound, with boards tied around their foreheads, leaving them with flat heads for the rest of their lives. Leeson experimented with his art, often merging and combining images in order to create special effects, and hand-colouring many of his photographs. Peter Grant relates in his book *Wish You Were Here: Life on Vancouver Island in Historical Photographs*, that Leeson's daughter, Anne, "would go down to meet the *Princess Maquinna* on her thrice-monthly visit to Winter Harbour and sell her father's postcards and pictures to tourists."[168]

Later, in 1937, Albert Moore established a logging float camp in Winter Harbour; it was taken over in the 1950s by his son Bill, who renamed it W.D. Logging. He painted his logging machinery a distinctive "salmon pink" colour. A well-read man who loved jazz, Moore wrote many articles in the BC *Lumberman* about life and logging on the west coast and coined the delightful term "Saltwater Main Street," referring to the BC coastal shipping routes of the CPR and Union Steamship vessels in the days before roads and airplanes. Bill's son Patrick, born here in 1947, became the co-founder and president of Greenpeace, spearheading protests against nuclear testing, whaling and seal-pup hunting in the 1970s and 1980s.

In one of his many articles, Bill recounts an incident following the logging camp's three-week Christmas closure, one January in the early 1940s. He and his boom man had stayed in camp, and he was due to meet the *Maquinna*, which was bringing in the twenty-five-man logging crew returning after the break:

By then our inlet had a small floating dock with a galvanized tin shed on it to store supplies out of the weather. There was no

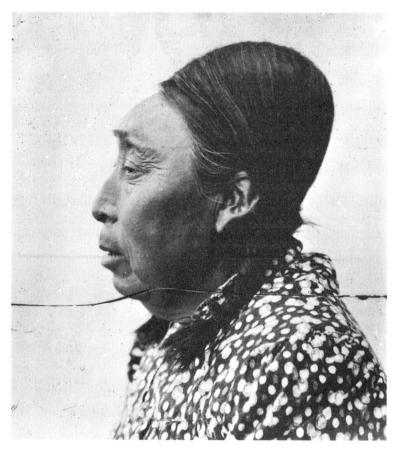

A Kwakiutl woman whose head was flattened in childhood. BEN LEESON
PHOTO, IMAGE VPL 14046 COURTESY OF THE VANCOUVER PUBLIC LIBRARY.

walkway to shore, so our dock sat out in sort of mid-channel, anchored to the bottom.

The "Good Ship" was due in at 4 a.m. (yes, it was snowing) and it was my job to meet her and take the crew and supplies farther up the inlet to the float camp. Fred, the boom man, was to have the bunkhouse wood fires going and to have lit the cookhouse wood range.

"Kelly" [Earle Kelly's radio program on CKCD radio] told me the night before when the ship would be in, so I slept aboard our gas boat ready to go out to the dock when she arrived. However, being young and heavy of sleep, I did not awaken as I should have and it was long after the "Good Ship" had departed that I was yelled at by a passing fisherman and told—"Ya got a whole passel of cranky loggers out there on the dock, kid."

I started up the engine and with a small searchlight on proceeded to the dock in the heavy snow. I shall never forget the sight of those 25 snow covered loggers—standing like penguins on the dock as my searchlight shone on them. Angry? No, they were way beyond that! The tin freight shed was full so there was no place to take cover. I had towed a large red cannery skiff behind my boat to load freight into. Twenty five cold loggers jumped at the freight to load it in the scow and about seven a.m. we headed up for the camp. To make the morning near perfect, Fred, the boom man had overslept and forgotten to light the fires. A couple of the loggers who would speak to me told me that their three day journey from Port Alberni had been one of the roughest on record for the "Good Ship"—Oh boy![169]

Pulling out of Winter Harbour, the *Maquinna* heads east through the tranquil waters of Quatsino Sound, a body of water so big it almost cuts off the top end of Vancouver Island, extending to within 7 miles (11 km) of the east coast of the Island. Soon the vessel arrives at the village of Quatsino. In 1894, thirty or so Norwegian farmers and their families arrived from North Dakota to take up eighty-acre land grants offered by the Canadian government. The settlement features a one-room schoolhouse, St. Olaf's church (built in 1897) and the Quatsino Hotel, which opened in 1912. In an article published in *The Islander* in 1980, writer I.M. Ildstad described how Captain Gillam often took the small liberty of leaving the ship for a brief period while in Quatsino.

While the *Princess Maquinna* was docked at the wharf the captain would frequently turn the unloading of freight over to his first officer and then walk about two miles [3 km] along a well-worn trail connecting the homes of the settlers to our own home. Here he and my father, Thomas, would have lively discussions on events of the time. These discussions were most enjoyable for my mother served them excellent coffee, home-made cake, and in season fresh strawberries and cream.[170]

"Captain Gillam was a popular man on the coast," adds Bill Moore, proceeding to describe a memorable event.

My friend, Frank Hole, remembers his days in the Quatsino school when, once a year, the captain would send word up to the teacher that he was ready to take the school children on board for a day's cruise of Quatsino Sound. Of course the great CPR service was theirs—from ice cream to white linen tablecloths and lovely silverware. Frank says it was the big day of the year.[171]

The *Maquinna* continues eastward, passing Ohlsen Point before turning into Quatsino Narrows. Once through into Holberg Inlet, she heads northeast to Coal Harbour on the east side of the inlet. Named after an unsuccessful mine founded here in 1883, Coal Harbour would later house a seaplane base during World War II. The float planes from Coal Harbour patrolled the Pacific searching for Japanese submarines and invasion fleets. After the base closed in 1945, the enterprising Gibson brothers, always on the lookout for any money-making opportunity, took over the base in 1948 and ran it as the last whaling station on the coast until they closed it in 1967.

In August 1907 this remote village gained notoriety when a syndicated story, first appearing in the Victoria *Times Colonist,* ran in newspapers across North America, including the *New York Times.* It asserted that John Sharp, the caretaker of the mining enterprise at Coal Harbour, was none other than William Quantrill, the leader of

The *Princess Maquinna* approaching the dock at Quatsino.

BEN LEESON PHOTO, IMAGE VPL 13919

COURTESY OF THE VANCOUVER PUBLIC LIBRARY.

the notorious Confederate guerilla group "Quantrill's Raiders." This renegade band included the notorious Dick Yeager, "Bloody Bill" Anderson, Jesse and Frank James, and the Younger brothers, and terrorized communities in Kansas and Missouri during the American Civil War. One notorious raid on Lawrence, Kansas, saw the gang massacre more than 150 people.

Toward the end of the war, after Union forces cut up his gang near Louisville, Kentucky, Quantrill was thought to have been killed. But according to the syndicated article, Quantrill survived a bullet and a bayonet stab and fled to South America, later making his way to northern Vancouver Island where he changed his name, logged, trapped and eventually became caretaker at the Coal Harbour mine facility. When in his cups, which occurred often, Sharp told his fellow drinkers that he was Quantrill, but not everyone believed him. However, in 1907 timber cruiser J.E. Duffy, who had been a Union cavalryman during the Civil War, came upon Sharp at Coal Harbour and identified him as Quantrill, an assertion Sharp did not deny.

The story goes that following the publication of the newspaper story, two men with American accents boarded the *Tees* in Victoria and arrived at Coal Harbour. Next day, Quatsino's Thomas Ildstad found Sharp suffering from the effects of a serious beating, but Sharp would not identify his assailants. He died the following day. The coroner who examined the body reportedly found evidence of many old wounds from bullets, swords and bayonets. The locals buried him in Coal Harbour. Later, during the building of the seaplane base during World War II, construction work obliterated the grave, and his true identity remains unresolved.

Travelling northwest along the length of Holberg Inlet, the *Maquinna* finally reaches the village of Holberg, the most northerly stop on her voyage, after sailing some 415 nautical miles (765 km) from Victoria. Danish settlers, who arrived here in 1895, named the village after Baron Ludvig Holberg, a noted Danish historian and dramatist. Some years later other hardy Scandinavians set off from Holberg, hiking to their ill-fated settlement at Cape Scott on the northwestern tip of Vancouver Island. The trek took them to San Josef Bay on the outer coast, where they followed a rugged trail to their settlement. Promises from the provincial government to build a wagon road to the settlement never materialized, but for years the settlers struggled to establish productive farms and gardens there, hoping to ship their produce to Victoria. Like so many other hopeful ventures on the west coast, the Cape Scott settlement eventually petered out.

On this voyage up the west coast, passengers have visited one remarkable garden—George Fraser's at Ucluelet. They have also heard about Cougar Annie's at Hesquiaht. Now here, about 9 miles (14.5 km) west of Holberg, lies another garden, created by Bernt

Ronning. Born in Norway, Ronning came to Canada in 1910 and in 1914 began homesteading 160 acres of land midway along the trail between Holberg and San Josef Bay. He built a house, trapped in winter, worked in summer at the Rivers Inlet salmon canneries and, as an expert chef, often served as cook in logging camps. His main interest, though, lay in buying seeds and shrubs from catalogues and planting them in the five-acre garden he had carved from the bush. In turn, he sold seeds and shrubs to others far and wide, all transported out on the *Princess Maquinna* and other CPR ships.

Two enormous monkey puzzle trees from Chile stood at the entrance to his garden, one eventually growing to over 80 ft (25 m) tall. Inside, peonies from China, rhododendrons and azaleas from India, yew and rowan trees from Ireland, heathers from Scotland, flowering cherries as well as oriental maples from the mountains of Japan, and many other species flourished in his garden. In 1951, Cecil Maiden noted how these species were all "thriving in the warm, moist air of his tropical valley, where winds are barred an entrance most of the year, and the soil is deep and inviting."[172]

No hermit, Ronning owned a pump organ and a gramophone and often hosted gatherings at his house where local folks enjoyed his fine refreshments and danced until first light. As dawn broke, the partygoers picked up their sleeping children spread round the house and walked back to their farms to feed, water and milk their cows.

Ronning maintained that the "best garden is the one outside my garden. There is nowhere else as bright with the wild flowers as these hillsides in spring."[173] He died in 1963. A small group of dedicated volunteers still tend his garden.

Business completed at Holberg, the *Maquinna* heads southeast down Holberg Inlet, through Quatsino Narrows, then steams some 7.5 nautical miles (14 km) southeast down Neroutsos Inlet, named after Captain Cyril D. Neroutsos, who succeeded Troup as superintendant of the CPR's shipping arm. About halfway down, on the west side of the inlet, the ship stops at Yreka, a copper mine boasting a store, blacksmith shop, sawmill, post office and bunkhouse/dining hall accommodating the sixty men who work there. As she nears the bottom end of the inlet, the *Maquinna* makes another stop, at Jeune Landing on the eastern shore, near where another copper mine operates, at one time employing thirty-five men. After a quick stop, the ship proceeds to the nearby company town of Port Alice, the biggest settlement in Quatsino Sound and the *Maquinna*'s final stop before beginning the return journey to Victoria.

Starting in 1917, the four Whalen brothers from Port Arthur, Ontario, founded the town to service the pulp mill they established there. Occupying sixty acres, the town had fifty homes, a hotel, a store, rooming houses and a sawmill—which it was claimed had the longest roof in the British Empire. The Whalens named the town after their mother, Alice. A good deal of the material used in building the town arrived aboard the *Maquinna*.

The town's 1,500 residents lived right next to the pulp mill's belching smokestacks and toxic outfall, which contributed to the degradation of the nearby water. Even the steamer contributed to the pollution, as long-time resident Eve Smith attested: "The *Maquinna*, having no refrigeration, brought live cattle to Port Alice to provide meat for the town and once they arrived they were slaughtered on the 'Oil Wharf,' with hay at one end and slaughter at the other, and the offal going into the chuck [the sea]."[174]

One of Captain Gillam's daughters, Irmgard—he had three daughters and a son—married Angus MacMaster in 1927 and they became residents of Port Alice in 1929. For two years, Captain Gillam made a number of visits to the MacMaster home when on the *Maquinna*'s regular runs, before his untimely death in May 1929.

John Steinbeck's friend Ed Ricketts, the famous botanist and ecologist, travelled on the *Maquinna* from Clayoquot to Port Alice in 1947, with his wife Toni. He left with a low opinion of the place. "Being a Saturday night, there was a dance and a social ashore. On the *Maquinna* ladies were prettying themselves for a night on

The Port Alice Pulp Mill, built in 1917 by Port Arthur's Whalen
brothers. They named the town after their mother, Alice.

IMAGE B-08103_141 COURTESY OF THE ROYAL BC MUSEUM.

the town." The merrymaking, however, fell far short of Ricketts's
expectations: "sad, sad dance, not at all like the peppy and drunken
country dances at Tofino," he complained. "These aren't, however,
wilderness people, or fishermen or farmers. They're townspeople
brought up here for a contract; they hate it and maybe they don't
even try very hard to have fun."[175]

While the passengers partied, work on the ship continued, with
the *Maquinna*'s winch operator, Shorty Wright, working overtime
when the ship stopped in Port Alice, loading bale after bale of pulp
into her holds for shipment to Victoria. On her return southward

The *Princess Maquinna* in heavy seas off Cape Scott.
IMAGE D-04329_142(1) COURTESY OF THE ROYAL BC MUSEUM.

journey, the *Maquinna* will stop again at many of the places she visited on her way north, filling her hold with all sorts of cargo for shipment and trans-shipment out of Victoria.

As gravel roads began linking Port Hardy, on the eastern side of the Island, to Holberg, Winter Harbour and Coal Harbour, and eventually a road connected Port Alice to Port McNeill in 1941, the *Maquinna* stopped making calls in Quatsino Sound. She also stopped making intermittent trips around Cape Scott at the top of the Island to Port Hardy and the east side of the Island. She sometimes carried First Nations people from the west side of Vancouver Island to Rivers Inlet on the mainland, for them to work in the canneries there. Over time, roads allowed the residents of these remote northern communities to travel east to Port Hardy and other ports on the east side of the Island. Once there, they could link with the Union Steamships vessels out of Vancouver on the "Saltwater Main Street" that served all the small communities between Vancouver and Prince Rupert. Those steamships made for a quicker journey to the "big smoke" and the bright city lights of Vancouver. However, losing the stops in Quatsino Sound proved to be the writing on the wall for the eventual demise of the CPR's West Coast service.

CHAPTER 16

HEADING SOUTH

EAVING THE confined and relatively calm waters of Quatsino Sound, the *Maquinna* often faced a more challenging trip heading south to Victoria than she did on her way north—especially in winter months. Southeast storms prevail on the coast in winter, so ships heading south have to plow straight into the teeth of these gales. This makes life decidedly uncomfortable for her passengers and crew. Inspector Brodie, in his 1918 report, wrote that: "The total distance from Victoria to Port Alice is 424 [nautical] miles [785 km], and of this distance the steamer travels in the open sea about 169 [nautical] miles [313 km], which would be about 15 hours of steaming in open water."[176] For those aboard the *Princess Maquinna*, especially those prone to seasickness, those hours could represent an eternity of suffering in tempestuous winter weather.

In his book *Beyond the Outer Shores*, Ucluelet-born Eric Enno Tamm uses Ed Ricketts's published and unpublished works to describe the ecologist's research on BC's west coast. In it he recounts Ed and Toni Ricketts's journey from Port Alice to Clayoquot in 1945, relating how quickly the transition from calm to storm could happen. The *Maquinna* stopped briefly just after leaving Port Alice, picking up two young fellows from a motorboat who were "working at liquor bottles." After they boarded "...the *Maquinna* then continued through the sheltered sound. Passengers lounged around the piano. Stewards were likely entertaining other passengers with seafaring tales. Tea was being served on the CPR's fine china. The two drunks kept swilling their whiskey. It was, at least for an hour or so, a quiet Sunday evening. Then the mood changed as the ship reached the open ocean," writes Ricketts.

Tamm continues: "A grim feeling immediately flooded the ship, a wave of seasickness. Many passengers became ghostly white. There was little appetite for dinner. 'Outside it got rough,' Ricketts wrote in his diary. 'We stood up forward as long as we could against the wind and spray, [and] then she started to take an occasional dash of water aboard.' He and the chief engineer tried to estimate the sweep of the mast. Ricketts figured it was fifteen, while the engineer thought twenty degrees. They were rounding Cape Cook, the eastern extremity on Brooks Peninsula, one of the most ruthless spots on the coast. The *Maquinna* squeaked and groaned in every joint as she rounded the stormy cape."

"A sleepless Ricketts stayed on deck," writes Tamm. "For a while, he was alone staring at 'wicked' Cape Cook and the gloomy gray combers crashing over the bow. One of the drunken men who had come aboard earlier appeared 'staggering and beastly.' A wave flung him across the deck and nearly overboard, as the ship pitched wildly. 'How are drunken people so saved?' Ricketts wondered. 'I guess he handled himself drunk better than I ever do sober.' Rounding the cape, the ocean quieted on the leeward side of the peninsula and Ricketts slipped below deck to get some rest."[177]

Any travel on the west coast by boat in a winter storm in open waters usually resulted in a rough ride. Lester Arellanes recalls a trip he took on the *Maquinna*:

A bunch of loggers, their wives and young unmarried men, clambered aboard (likely at Nootka Cannery): they had been drinking. In the alleged saloon on the *Maquinna* was about a three-quarter keyboard piano, not far from my stateroom. That piano had weathered as many storms as the *Maquinna* had, and it was terribly out of tune, but that gang got the piano hooked up, and they were dancing and laughing and talking. We had cast off and had turned around and were heading out of Nootka Sound; we had to go outside, until we passed Estevan Point. These guys were whooping it up and playing this little piano for all it would stand... Within five minutes after we stuck our noses outside, they were GONE. No more piano, no more laughter, no more gaiety. It was all over. The Captain later told me that we were having gusts up to 80 miles [130 km] an hour and it was blowing between 50 and 60 knots steadily outside.[178]

Adding to the perils of west coast travel, no matter what route being travelled, or in what direction the ship was heading, was fog. In the late summer and fall, fog plagues the west coast, to the point that locals sometimes refer to August as "Fogust." In the days before radar, sonar and the Global Positioning System (GPS), navigating the coast demanded extraordinary skills of ships' captains to avoid catastrophes. Advection fog, as it is called, occurs when warm air, coming from the land, condenses when it contacts colder air over the sea. It becomes so thick that visibility falls to around 65 ft (20 m). Over the years, the *Maquinna*'s captain, Edward Gillam, like all other seasoned steamer captains on the coast, found ways to navigate safely in the thickest fog without ever having to alter the ship's speed or schedule.

The captains knew they could depend on the meticulous logs they kept of every journey, in both good and bad weather, noting every change of course and the exact time it took to travel each section of that course. On CPR ships three log books remained open on the bridge at all times: the log in which the bridge crew were currently making entries, the log of the previous voyage, and the one from the previous year. The bridge crew also noted exactly the speed at which the ship travelled and every hazard she encountered. This meant that when they travelled in fog they could effectively see in the dark.

These navigators also knew the routes they travelled like the backs of their hands: some even drew outlines of the nearby mountains into their log books so that at night the mountain outlines, sometimes dimly visible against the night sky, would help them pinpoint their location. "Those old timers were real 'seamen' because they were outside on the bridge in all weathers and understood the elements," says David Young, long-time skipper of the *Uchuck III*, the freight/passenger ship that still plies the west coast out of Gold River. He also points out that when travelling at night, or in fog, all lights on the bridges of coastal steamers, save for the small light in the binnacle, remained unlit. No one smoked on the bridge, for even the light from a cigarette tip might diminish the skipper's or helmsman's view.

Like a blind person with a cane, the whole secret of making way in fog depended on sound. Steam engines like the *Princess Maquinna*'s made far less noise than modern diesel engines, giving captains a far greater ability to hear what they needed to hear. They knew exactly how to listen, with a watch in their hands. Knowing sound travels at the rate of 1,126 ft (343 m) per second or about 5.5 seconds per mile (3 seconds per km), they would sound the ship's whistle and wait for an echo. If the blast of the ship's whistle took 11 seconds for the echo to return from the land, they knew that whatever object the sound echoed back from would be a mile (1.6 km) away—5.5 seconds to reach shore and the same again to return. The skippers also knew the different sounds echoes made when they bounced back from the land. "They knew that a long sandy spit gives an echo with a distinct hiss, a rocky cliff gives a very clear echo, thick forest produces a muffled echo, and where there is a little island off a head [headland] you'll get a double echo,"[179] commented veteran CPR captain Archibald Phelps. Margaret Horsfield, in *Voices from the Sound*, records what another old hand, Captain W.J. Boyce, wrote in a 1923 article about the primary requirement for navigating the fog, which is:

"a thorough mental photograph of the coast on the course the ship is taking. As the vessel proceeds the navigator must picture the shore as it slips by. Perhaps he cannot see further than the ship's bow with his eyes. But with his ears he is seeing everything necessary within a couple of miles. At his hand he has the steam siren." He describes in detail how the echoes change as the land around changes, that "a two-second echo return from abaft the beam" means that the channel is open ahead and he has passed the nearest point of land; or that when the echoes become "splendidly equalized" he is right in the middle of a narrow channel. Yet echoes can also be confusing; the shores can send back unwelcome and unexpected sounds, especially in narrow inlets, where sound bounces back and forth. For coastal captains, however, nothing challenged them more than thick blinding snow, for in such conditions sound is muffled, and the echoes can't speak at all.[180]

Captain Gillam knew well the dangers of navigating in snow. In January 1911, while skippering the *Tees* on her way south from Ucluelet across Barkley Sound, the vessel hit Gowlland Islet at night during a heavy snowstorm. As a safety precaution, he off-loaded all of his passengers by lifeboat to the whaling station at Sechart for the night. No one suffered any injuries but the ship's bow suffered a dent that had to be repaired when the ship returned to Victoria.

In skippering both the *Tees* and the *Maquinna* Captain Gillam gained a breadth of experience that served him well as he navigated the west coast. As "Old Timer" wrote in a 1955 article in the *Western Advocate*: "One foggy day after he slowly and silently nosed the *Maquinna* into Refuge Cove, a tricky and narrow entrance, a passenger remarked to him at dinner 'My, we went into that place very quietly.' The captain agreed, saying 'I was waiting for those dogs to bark in order to get my bearings.'"[181] A good captain knew all the sounds to expect: roosters, chickens, dogs, as well as whistle buoys, and sounds from creeks and gravel beaches. "Captain Gillam's ability to navigate in fog was legendary, not only on the west coast but elsewhere. Once when the *Maquinna* travelled to Vancouver, English Bay lay enveloped in thick fog and crowded with vessels at anchor, none of them daring to move—not even the large *Empress* ships with local pilots on board—Gillam and the *Maquinna* arrived precisely on time, entirely untroubled by the fog. One of the pilots wryly said to him afterwards, 'Did you have to do that to us?'"[182]

The *Maquinna*'s southbound trip takes her back to some of the places she stopped at on her northern journey. On our 1924 trip she stops again at Chamiss Bay, picking up loggers going to the bright lights and beer parlours of the city where, as Ian Tyson would sing decades later in his song "Summer Wages," "...the dreams of a season are all spilled down on the floor."[183] Many of them will likely return to Chamiss Bay, or to other logging camps, within a week or two having blown all of their hard-earned money in the city.

As she continues south, the *Maquinna* stops at Cachalot, where she loads whale oil and ground bone meal for trans-shipment out of Victoria. Passengers will board at Nootka Cannery, and skid loads of canned salmon will be swung into the hold. At Ahousaht she will load shingles and cut lumber from the Gibsons' sawmill as well as passengers heading south. Here too, in late summer and early fall, whole families of Ahousaht people will begin the first stage of their annual journey to the hops fields of Puyallup County in Washington State, where they will pick that important crop used for making beer. From Clayoquot and Tofino she will welcome passengers, and maybe those already aboard will disembark for an impromptu dance at Tofino's community hall, particularly if a wedding is taking place. Later the honeymooners will join the ship for their first night as a married couple. At Ucluelet she will pick up more passengers as well as packages of seeds and cuttings from George Fraser's garden being shipped to his customers far and wide. Port Alberni will see her load lumber, coal and passengers, and at Kildonan cases of salmon and barrels of pilchard oil will be lowered into the hold. Bamfield brings the possibility of another dance at the telegraph station, while the coal and lumber, loaded in Port Alberni, will be off-loaded. At Port Renfrew yet more passengers will join the ship for the short hop to Victoria. The *Maquinna* only stops "as required" as it steams southward, based on requests made on the journey north and standing orders for collection of cargo, while passing places that offer her "no trade."

Going south she might carry expectant mothers heading to Victoria to have their babies, as was common on the coast in those days; or people with medical issues who need hospital treatment in Tofino, Port Alberni or Victoria. Whatever the needs of the people of the west coast, the *Maquinna*, her captain and crew dealt with any and all eventualities.

The *Maquinna* usually arrives back in Victoria in the early morning, and the crew immediately begins off-loading the cargo holds. The passengers, having cleared their cabins, descend the gangway and disperse through the terminal, heading out onto Belleville Street. The seas of the west coast lie behind them, and the tourists among them will talk about the week-long trip for the rest of their lives.

Once she is off-loaded, the crew immediately begins preparing the ship for her next week-long journey, loading food for the dining room, filling the bunkers with oil, sending the laundry to be cleaned and picking up fresh. The deck crew will begin loading the ship's holds with a host of orders for westcoasters that will have been gathering in the CPR's Belleville Street warehouse. Among the items will be grocery orders from the Woodward's store in Vancouver that have been brought across the Strait of Georgia to Victoria on the CPR ships that serve those routes (occasionally, the *Maquinna* would make a run to Vancouver herself to pick up goods, most likely at night so as not to disturb her timetable). Items ordered from the Eaton's catalogue will also be waiting to be loaded, as well as a host of other materials needed by logging outfits, miners, fishermen, boat builders and machinists.

Preparations will continue all day at the busy dock, and in the evening of the following day new passengers will begin arriving, keen to be aboard before the ship sails at 11 p.m. Then the *Maquinna* will set out on another west coast run, continuing the seemingly never-ending cycle of travel up and down the coast, providing the service essential to so many westcoasters in their isolated communities.

CHAPTER 17

TOURISM AND TRAGEDY

MANY MAY THINK of west coast tourism as a fairly recent phe-
nomenon. Visitors have flocked to the west coast of Vancouver
Island since the road to Tofino was punched through from Port
Alberni in 1959, with even more following as the road
improved, and yet more flooding in after the Pacific Rim National
Park, protecting land on both sides of Barkley Sound, was established in 1971. The intense international coverage of the Clayoquot
Sound logging protests of 1993 brought even more visitors, and since
then they have come in ever-increasing numbers, making Tofino one
of the leading tourist destinations in Canada. However, this urge to
visit the west coast is far from new, and long pre-dates our group of
tourists disembarking in Victoria after their seven-day cruise aboard
the *Maquinna* in 1924. The steamship companies serving the coast
catered to this tourist market almost from their inception—they even
helped to create it.

The opportunity to sail up the west coast of BC on an adventurous cruise had fired the imagination of travellers for decades before
our 1924 trip. In 1888 California's Pacific Coast Steamship Company launched the successful Alaska cruise industry with monthly
voyages to southeastern Alaska from San Francisco, later joined by
the Alaska Steamship Company trips from Seattle. Travelling the

The CPR used coloured posters to promote its Sunset Cruises, often using images of totem poles, First Nations people paddling canoes and women weaving and selling baskets, despite the fact that Indigenous people were not welcome in the interiors of its vessels. IMAGES FROM 93-7330 EARL MARSH ACCESSION BOX 3, COURTESY OF THE ROYAL BC MUSEUM.

SUNSET CRUISES to the

West Coast

OF VANCOUVER ISLAND

AND SPECIAL 7-DAY
CRUISE AROUND
VANCOUVER ISLAND

1936

Canadian Pacific
B.C. COAST SERVICE

Canadian Pacific
B.C. COAST SERVICE

west coast of Vancouver Island had already become a recreational event, when the Canadian Pacific Navigation Company advertised in the *Colonist* in 1886 "that excursionists could travel to Clayoquot on the little steamer *Maude*." Soon after the launch of the *Maquinna* in 1913, the CPR began tentatively promoting the attractions of the west coast for recreational travellers. Inspector H.W. Brodie hinted at the potential of the tourist trade on his inspection trip in 1918, and what the company could do to prepare for it: "If we decide to go in for additional tourist business during June, July, August and September, the service can be slightly improved. A few deck chairs are required, a phonograph for dancing, and an awning over the after deck. A bath room or two would require to be provided."[184]

In the 1920s and 1930s the company went all-out to promote its Sunset Cruises, publishing vividly coloured brochures replete with images of totem poles, of First Nations people paddling canoes and of Indigenous women weaving baskets. Such marketing capitalized on the images and skills of people generally not allowed entry into the interior of any of the CPR ships on the West Coast run. Whether or not this was company policy, First Nations people routinely travelled up the coast on deck and in the hold, while white passengers had far better accommodation. This stark contrast seems to have generated scant reaction or comment at the time. Most tourists travelling on the Sunset Cruises aboard the *Maquinna* likely paid little attention to how the First Nations or Asian passengers were accommodated on the ships, being absorbed in their own adventure aboard. The cruises proved so popular that in the summer, locals living on the west coast often loudly complained of not being able to find accommodation on the ship, because all the staterooms were taken by tourists.

In the summer months during the 1930s and 1940s, tourists could take a seven-day cruise all the way up the west coast to Holberg in Quatsino Sound and back to Victoria or Seattle for as little as $39, including the cost of a berth and meals.

SUNSET CRUISES

TO THE
WEST COAST
OF
VANCOUVER ISLAND

Sailings from Victoria, B.C., 11.00 p.m.

"PRINCESS NORAH"
June 1 - 11 - 21 ◆ **July 6 - 16 - 26**
August 6 - 16 - 24 ◆ **Sept. 1 - 11 - 21**

"PRINCESS MAQUINNA"
July 1 - 11 - 21 ◆ **August 1 - 11 - 21**

- 6½ days delightful cruising along the rugged scenic West Coast of Vancouver Island.

- Minimum return fare from Victoria, $42.90 (Berth and meals included.) Children, five years of age and under twelve, will be charged half minimum fare, plus full premium (if any.)

- Passengers leave Vancouver on 10:30 a.m. steamer, day of cruise, returning to Vancouver from Victoria either 1:45 p.m. or 12 midnight steamers, day of arrival of West Coast Steamship at Victoria.

- Every facility and comfort is available on both the "Princess Norah" and "Princess Maquinna" to make these Sunset Cruises most memorable and enjoyable.

- Unparalleled Meal Service.

- ROMANCE AND HISTORY ABOUND ON THE WEST COAST. See for yourself these historic points, which Captain James Cook discovered late in the Seventeenth Century.

The CPR's west coast route attracted ever-increasing tourist traffic in the 1920s, too much for the *Princess Maquinna* to handle. The company built the *Princess Norah* in response to this demand. IMAGE FROM 93-7330 EARL MARSH ACCESSION BOX 3, COURTESY OF THE ROYAL BC MUSEUM.

Popular demand for these cruises grew to the point that in 1928 Superintendent James Troup contracted Fairfield Shipbuilding Company on the Clyde, in Scotland, to build the *Princess Norah*—the last *Princess* ship Troup would build before he retired. Troup, who commanded the respect and affection of all, retired in September 1928, before the *Norah*'s maiden voyage in April 1929. Captain Cyril D. Neroutsos replaced him as superintendent. Known as "the Skipper," Neroutsos was born in England and came to Seattle as a first mate on the *Garonne*, later moving to Victoria where he joined the Canadian Pacific Navigation Company before it was taken over by the CPR. Like Troup, Neroutsos had a keen interest in ship design and canny insight into the workings of coastal shipping.

The arrival of the *Norah* showed the commitment of the company to the tourist trade, hinted at by Inspector Brodie a decade earlier. And yes, the *Norah* would have deck chairs, awnings over the aft deck, baths and even showers.

The *Princess Norah* would be a thousand gross tons heavier than the *Maquinna,* but her length would be comparable, so she could continue using the existing wharves on the west coast. Both more manoeuvrable and more luxurious than the *Maquinna,* the *Norah* would run on the west coast of Vancouver Island in summer and to Alaska in winter. "Her larger superstructure housed more elaborate accommodation, which included a large observation lounge on the upper deck forward, and an attractive smoking room aft. The dining saloon could seat 100. Her 61 staterooms had 165 berths; they included four large deluxe rooms with private baths and 14 other cabins with showers."[185]

Her inaugural voyage, with Captain Gillam in command, left Victoria on April 7, 1929, with the Governor General of Canada and his wife, Lord and Lady Willingdon, aboard. Also on this voyage were the Hon. Randolph Bruce, the Lieutenant-Governor of BC, and an array of dignitaries. Their arrival at the various stops en route caused a great stir among the locals:

At Bamfield the residents turned out en masse to greet the representatives of His Majesty. Lord Willingdon was shown around the cable station and sent out cables to Sir Basil Blackett and Sir Campbell Stewart. At Ucluelet the *Norah* was invaded by school-children of three races, white, Indians, and Japanese who had been accorded a holiday for the occasion. Boatloads of Indians, in native attire, swarmed around the *Norah* as she came in. In Tofino, Indians in ceremonial attire, with painted faces and traditional headgear, tendered a formal reception to the vice-regal visitors at a colorful ceremony—which included the investiture of Lord Willingdon with the rank of Chieftain of the Clayoquot tribe. Numerous Indian baskets, carved Indian canes, and interesting totem poles of black slate, as well as two fish weighing more than 100 pounds each, were presented and which the passengers enjoyed for lunch the next day.[186]

The *Norah* took her passengers as far north as Port Alice before returning to Victoria.

The *Norah*'s second west coast trip proved to be Captain Gillam's last. Then aged 65, he apparently suffered a fit of dizziness while on his way from his quarters and fell down a companionway, suffering fatal injuries. He died on board. When the sad news reached the various settlements on the west coast, everyone felt the loss keenly, for Gillam was loved and respected by all. "I remember my mother saying afterwards that he must have fallen because he was not yet used to the layout of the different vessel," says Tony Guppy. "I was struck by the terrible irony: after all the years he had navigated one of the world's most treacherous stretches of water, he died in a fall aboard a voyage ship."[187]

"Captain Gillam, Purser Cornelius and the officers of the *Maquinna* were the best public relations group the CPR ever had," wrote "Old Timer" in the *Western Advocate* in 1955. "Many times when the *Maquinna* would be unloading cargo all night, Capt. Gillam would

This poignant Ben Leeson photograph of the *Princess Norah* at the Quatsino dock in early May 1929 bears the note "with her dead master." Captain Edward Gillam, long-time captain of the *Princess Maquinna*, had died a few days earlier at Tofino after taking over the captaincy of the *Princess Norah*. She continued her scheduled northward journey to Quatsino and Holberg before turning south, carrying Gillam back to where he would be buried in Ross Bay Cemetery. IMAGE VPL 13935 COURTESY OF THE VANCOUVER PUBLIC LIBRARY.

organize a dance in the main saloon, furniture would be shoved aside and 'joy' would be unrestrained. Many a pleasant night I spent chasing 'Madam Terpsichore' [the Greek muse of dance] on the *Maquinna*."[188]

"Captain Gillam's calm authority and his good nature were as famous as his seamanship," writes Margaret Horsfield in *Voices from the Sound*:

He could control a group of drunken loggers with a glance. And, according to Mike Hamilton, the prospectors were even worse than the loggers: 'Seldom did the coast steamer sail north or south without having aboard a number of miners and prospectors either coming or going. They were usually a rough, tough bunch, frequently hard drinkers with a vocabulary, when in their cups, capable of making anyone's hair curl.' But Captain Gillam could be counted on to keep the atmosphere on board his ship amiable, and he always ensured the well-being of the ladies on board.

Gillam served as captain of the *Maquinna* with dedication and unflappable calm throughout the 1910s and 1920s. Combined with his earlier service on board other vessels, he navigated the West Coast on the coastal steamers for some thirty years, witnessing at close quarters the changes in all the settlements on the coast... He saw the demise of sealing, the heyday of the West Coast whaling industry, and later, by the mid 1920s, its end. He saw small mines open and close and small sawmills flourish and fade. He saw the end of the hand logging era on the coast and the coming of mechanization, the beginning of the massive pilchard fishery, the beginning of the pulp and paper industry as mills opened at Port Alice, Alberni and Tahsis... He saw the scheduled stops along the West Coast steamer route increase year by year to serve the ever changing industries and settlements on the coast. Through their cargo, he knew every single development on the coast and all the people involved: the powerful Gibson family at their successful shingle mill at Ahousaht, the struggling Rae-Arthur family trying to operate a nursery garden at their remote Boat Basin homestead, the storekeepers, the schools and every one of the native Indians selling their baskets and handicrafts at Tofino and Nootka and Kyuquot.[189]

"Old Timer" also wrote about Captain Gillam's ability to keep order aboard his ship, despite any "excitement or feverish haste" among the prospectors. "I don't remember one bad incident happening during that time. I believe some of the bad boys took one look at Capt. Gillam and decided that if they played him it would be for keeps."[190]

The *Maquinna* and Captain Gillam answered countless emergency calls to help save a life or help with a birth. He would hasten the *Maquinna* to the nearest of three hospitals, one at Port Alice, another in Tofino and the other at Port Alberni. His acts of kindness made him legendary on the west coast.

Port Gillam on Vargas Island, Gillam Channel in Esperanza Inlet and the Gillam Islands in Quatsino Sound all bear Captain Gillam's name. He lies buried in Ross Bay Cemetery in Victoria.

Captain Robert "Red" Thompson, "thickset and broad shouldered, a ruddy complexion beneath a head of hair that was once red but is now mellowing to white,"[191] took over as captain of the *Maquinna* following Gillam's death. From the Shetland Islands, where he worked with his father from the age of 14 on sailing schooners fishing in the North Sea, he came to Canada in 1898, where he joined the Canadian Pacific Navigation Company as an able seaman. Later he joined the Canadian Pacific Coast fleet and served as an officer or captain on twelve of its fourteen passenger ships. In summer, when the *Princess Norah* returned to the west coast for the tourist season, Red Thompson took over its captaincy, and William "Black" Thompson—no relation—became skipper of the *Princess Maquinna*. Black Thompson had been captain of the *Princess Charlotte* and *Princess Elaine* prior to working on both the *Princess Norah* and *Princess Maquinna*.

Red Thompson would continue as captain of the *Maquinna*—off and on—until he "swallowed the anchor" and retired in 1944. He became a familiar and well-liked figure to all who sailed with him, earning him the title of "West Coast Skipper." Subsequent captains of the *Maquinna* included Black Thompson, Martin MacKinnon, Leonard McDonald, Ralph Carthew and Peter Leslie.

Over the years, the *Princess Maquinna* carried a wide variety of passengers and a great deal of unpredictable cargo. For the tourists

Officers "Pr.Maquinna" late 1930's.S.G.Hunter,1st Officer;A.N.McDonald,2nd Officer;B.Scott,Purser, Fred McGraw,Chief Engr; Capt.Martin MacKinnon (cap over eyes).James Eddie,3rd Officer;Percy Trowsdale,3rd Engr. Marconi operator ?

Captain Red Thompson, referred to as the "West Coast Skipper," took over the captaincy of the *Princess Maquinna* following Captain Gillam's death. IMAGE J-08080 COURTESY OF THE ROYAL BC MUSEUM.

Captain Martin MacKinnon and his officers on the *Princess Maquinna*. IMAGE J-08079 COURTESY OF THE ROYAL BC MUSEUM.

aboard the *Maquinna* and the *Norah,* watching the deck crews carefully winch up and off-load the huge variety of cargo from the ship's holds at their various stops proved an endless source of fascination.

The *Daily Colonist* reported in March 1925 that the *Maquinna* was taking a consignment of muskrats on her trip north. "They were trapped along the Fraser River, and are being shipped up the west coast to be put ashore at Quatsino Sound, where it is hoped they will multiply and eventually provide a lucrative fur industry for Victoria."[192] Another time, a horse found its way aboard the *Maquinna,* not into one of the holds or onto the foredeck, where livestock usually travelled, but into a cabin. "The horse was snuck aboard one night while the ship was in Victoria," Tom Henry relates in *Westcoasters.* "The culprits led the nag, head first, into the cabin, then departed and shut the door. When an unusual stink led a crewman to the cabin, there was turmoil. Any thought of reversing the horse out of the cabin was abandoned after a few bone-shattering lashes with its hooves. In the end, the cabin wall was cut away and the horse let out."[193]

People on the west coast relied on the *Maquinna* to deliver their standard household supplies. "We used to get stuff from Woodward's in Vancouver," says Ucluelet's Margaret Warren. "My mother would send her order to the CPR Office in Victoria and the *Maquinna* would go to Vancouver and pick up everyone's orders from Woodward's. The *Maquinna* charged only $2-$3 freight for shipping 10-11 boxes—a month's supply. It didn't matter if you were short of money, you'd just pay the next time."[194]

Johnnie Vanden Wouwer tells the same story, from Bamfield:

> About once a month, we used to get an order of groceries on the *Maquinna*, around $10 or $20 worth, from Woodward's in Vancouver. You'd get butter that way, in bulk, fourteen pounds of butter. And Peanut butter and honey, too, in big containers. Woodward's own brand. We knew when the boat was coming, of course, and we'd row over there to the Cable Station and sometimes it came during a storm. And hundred pound sacks of chicken wheat, I'll never forget them![195]

Even though there were few roads in west coast communities, residents with extra money still bought cars and other vehicles that had to be carried up the coast on the *Maquinna*. In order to load them, the *Maquinna*'s crew devised special slings to hoist the vehicles on and off the deck and in and out of holds. "We copied those slings," says David Young, former skipper of the *Uchuck III*, the coastal freighter that still operates out of Gold River. "It was a system of bars that locked around the front and back wheels of the vehicle and a cage affair hanging from the cargo hook with wires in all four corners that fastened onto hooks on the outside ends of the bars ... Those slings are still being used on our boat to this day."[196]

Even today tourists travelling aboard the *Uchuck III* and the *Frances Barkley* on the west coast continue to be fascinated by the off-loading of cargo, just as the tourists aboard the *Maquinna* and *Norah* were a century ago.

CHAPTER 18

WARTIME ON
THE WEST COAST

I N AUGUST 1914, at the outbreak of World War I, the *Princess Maquinna* carried many west coast volunteers to Victoria on the first leg of their journey to the battlefields of Europe. Many were Britons who had recently arrived as settlers, and they rushed to defend Britain and the Empire. They enlisted from Quatsino, Vargas Island, Tofino, Ucluelet and nearly every community on the coast. Many of them would never return, leaving widows and children. Clo-oose was particularly hard hit, suffering eleven casualties of the thirty-one who joined up. The tiny community held the distinction of having the highest rate of enlistment per capita of any community in Canada.

Twenty-five years later, on September 10, 1939, when Canada declared war on Germany to begin its participation in World War II, the announcement did not bring the same rush of west coast enlistment. Canada's attachments to Britain and the Empire were no longer as strong as in 1914.

Everything changed on December 7, 1941, however, when Japanese forces attacked the US Pacific fleet at Pearl Harbor, Hawaii, 2,300 nautical miles (4,200 km) to the west of Vancouver Island. Almost overnight a sense of panic hit the coast of British Columbia. Suddenly the Canadian government and the people living on the coast realized how unprotected they were from a potential Japanese attack. Only two Canadian naval vessels and a few ancient aircraft stood ready to defend the whole of the West Coast of Canada from a Japanese invasion. Canada's Western Air Command immediately began upgrading its amphibious air base at Ucluelet so the outdated Stranraer and Shark "flying boats," as the military called them, could better patrol the Pacific looking for submarines and possible invasion fleets. Construction also began on a new amphibious air base at Coal Harbour in Quatsino Sound. As well, work began on a wheeled aircraft base at Tofino to enable more, and bigger, aircraft to patrol the coast. The Tofino air base opened in October 1942. These large building projects brought many people to the west coast, but did not result in any notable increase in traffic for the *Maquinna*. The air bases in Ucluelet and Tofino relied on small, local freight/passenger vessels such as the *Lady Rose* and the *Uchuck I* to supply them out of Port Alberni. In 1941 a gravel road had been finished connecting Coal Harbour on Quatsino Sound to Port McNeill on the east side of the Island, where the Union Steamship Company's vessels provided fast and frequent service to and from Vancouver, making the building of the air base at Coal Harbour a much more manageable project.

With these projects moving forward, many west coast fishermen joined the Fishermen's Reserve, which became familiarly known as the "Gumboot Navy." They took their fishboats to Victoria where the captains and crew underwent basic training, and the Royal Canadian Navy (RCN) fitted the boats with .303 Lewis machine guns, wireless/telegraph sets and depth charges. The "Gumboot Navy" would patrol the coast throughout the war looking for suspicious activity and assisting the RCN whenever called upon.

Other westcoasters joined the Pacific Coast Military Rangers, also known as the BC Rangers. These loggers, trappers, prospectors and First Nations volunteers living in remote locations also kept an eye out for suspicious activities.

During World War II over 2,000 air force and 8,000 army
personnel, as well as 80 members of the Woman's Division, served
at the Tofino and Ucluelet air bases. Here aircrew at Tofino pose
with a Bolingbroke bomber in 1944. IMAGE PA 162822 COURTESY
OF LIBRARY AND ARCHIVES CANADA.

In early 1942, following the Pearl Harbor attack, the *Maquinna*
sailed to Vancouver to receive a coat of wartime camouflage paint.
Historian Jan Peterson records the recollections of crewman Geoff
Wyman:

The *Maquinna* arrived in Vancouver at 11 a.m. and was fully painted
battleship gray in time to leave that evening. Unfortunately, the
funnel was still hot when it was painted, so by the time it was out
to sea, the paint had turned a bright silver making it more visible
than ever. Wyman also remembered that a big gun [a 12-pounder]
was mounted on the stern of the vessel. The idea being that the
ship, which was faster than most warships, would steam away, and
with the gun at the stern, could take shots at ships or U Boats pur-
suing it.[197]

The *Princess Maquinna* in drab, grey camouflage
paint during World War II. MAURICE CHANDLER PHOTO.
COURTESY OF THE ROBERT D. TURNER COLLECTION.

After the initial flurry of wartime preparations, the Canadian government decided that the 23,000 Japanese Canadians living on or near the coast in British Columbia posed a security threat. Rumours circulated that some of the Japanese fishermen were members of the Japanese imperial forces, and would likely help the enemy in the event of an invasion of BC. Almost immediately after Pearl Harbor, during December 1941 and January 1942, the RCN seized every fishboat owned by Japanese fishermen on the coast and took them, or had them taken, to New Westminster. Then in February 1942, the Canadian government passed an Order in Council ordering all Japanese residents in BC be interned a minimum of 100 miles (160 km) from the coast.

For the hundreds of Japanese living in coastal Vancouver Island communities this upheaval caused tremendous pain and heartache. Over the years living on the west coast, they had become respected members of their communities; their children attended local schools; they were enthusiastic participants in local events and generous contributors to community endeavours. All of this made no difference. The order came in March 1942 that all Japanese residents must be prepared to leave their homes in forty-eight hours.

On the morning of March 15, 1942, twenty-seven Japanese people from Clayoquot and sixty-eight from Tofino assembled at the government wharf waiting for the *Princess Maquinna*, which did not arrive until late in the day. Looking out from her window over the crowded wharf, Katie Monks worried about the long wait they were enduring. "I said 'Harold ... there isn't even a public toilet over there and the women and all those kids—could I go over and get some of them and bring them over here and at least give them a cup of tea?' Her husband thought about it quite a while because it was bothering us. He finally said, 'Well, I don't think you should. Just look at it this way: they're leaving but we have to stay.'"[198]

The *Maquinna* eventually arrived, looking "drab and ominous in her wartime grey," and the Japanese embarked with their suitcases and bundles. "Not one of them looked back and not one of them waved goodbye ... I never heard their departure discussed—ever— by children in my age group, or by the adults."[199]

The Canadian government interned a total of 23,000 Japanese during World War II, including a number of veterans from the previous war. During the 1914-18 war 222 Japanese Canadians had fought for Canada; 54 had died and 11 won the Military Medal for bravery. The overall number of Japanese evacuees also included 231 Japanese from Ucluelet and 19 from Bamfield. They received their evacuation notice on March 20, 1942, five days after the Japanese of Tofino and Clayoquot had been taken away.

On the night of June 20, 1942, when a Japanese submarine—or perhaps some other vessel—shelled Estevan Lighthouse at the north end of Clayoquot Sound, the incident further heightened the fear of those living on the west coast. Even though the incident remains debatable to this day, its impact proved dramatic, bringing the war right to the doorstep of west coast residents and sparking widespread alarm. According to Neil Robertson:

> On that date a Japanese submarine, reported to be the *I-26*, surfaced 2 miles [3.2 km] off Estevan Point and fired about 25 rounds of 5.5″ shells at the Estevan Point lighthouse. Most fell short, but some went over the lighthouse and into the village of Hesquiaht. At the time a number of rumors went around concerning the incident. There were reports of other ships in the area at the time including Navy ships. One account was that the shells were fired by a US Navy ship and another was that it was a Canadian Navy ship, ordered to do so by the Prime Minister, W.L. Mackenzie King, in order to stir up the population and get support for his conscription policy.[200]

Various theories and rumours spread about what really happened at Estevan Point. Heightened stories along the coast at times verged on the unbelievable, even comical. Tofino's Bjarne Arnet served as a skipper in the Fishermen's Volunteer Reserve at the time of the Estevan Lighthouse shelling and he received orders over his radio to take his boat out and intercept the submarine. On board he had three old Enfield rifles from World War I and a stripped down Lewis gun. Having been born and raised in Tofino he knew every shoal, rock and sandbar on the coast, but decided to take no chances on this mission. "The next thing you know," recalled a fellow Fishermen's Reserve member, "Esquimalt got a message from Bjarne that they were 'aground on a sandbar!' No way was he going after a sub equipped like that!"[201]

Neil Robertson recorded another funny story of the Estevan Lighthouse incident that possesses all the elements of a good west coast yarn—without a shred of evidence to support it. Unsurprisingly it involves the indomitable and mischievous Gordon Gibson and the *Princess Maquinna*. "Early in the war a gun had been mounted on the *Maquinna* and a Royal Canadian Navy gunner was posted to the ship to man it and train some crewmembers in its use. The story goes that

Gordon Gibson was aboard and had been partying with some friends. While off Estevan Point he and his friends fired the shots from the deck gun. Some years later Mr. Gibson was questioned about the incident at his Maui Lu Resort on Maui and he vociferously denied it. There is no mention of the incident in the *Maquinna*'s Log."²⁰²

Throughout the war the *Maquinna* continued her faithful service on the west coast, camouflaged in her grey paint. Despite the war, her work carried on normally, back and forth, up and down the coast, with occasional forays to Vancouver. A few samples from the CPR files indicate some of her more notable wartime moments.

Oct. 27th / 1940. David Beatty of Estevan Pt. B.C. embarked on this ship as passenger at Ahousat B.C. about midnight October 26th 1940, and was berthed in Room No. 27. He said he was not feeling well and asked for tea and sandwiches in his room. At about 3:45 am the night steward reported him dead in his room. The Provincial Police from P.M.L. No. 14, which was in port at the time, took charge of the remains. R. Thompson, Master.

Oct. 23 / 1941, 6:45 am. 1st Narrows, Vancouver Harbour. Outbound for Victoria, collided with West Vancouver Ferryboat *Hollyburn* inbound through first narrows in dense fog. Both ships were proceeding dead slow and had only a few passengers. Only damage was to the railings of the *Hollyburn*. W. Thompson, Master.

Jan. 22 / 1942, 6:39 am. Ship touched bottom in Alberni Inlet in Lat. 49-09-21N Long. 124-45-27W in dense fog. No damage. R. Thompson, Master.

Oct. 3rd / 1942, 11:15 a.m. On arrival at Vancouver on Oct 3rd, city detectives boarded the ship and arrested Robert Gerrie, aged 20, Canadian, Messboy, and Norman R. Woodland, aged 21, Canadian, night Saloon man, charging them with theft committed ashore. Joined 24-9-42, taken off 3-10-42. R. Thompson, Master.

Nov 25 / 1942. Vilko Virta, age 51 years, native of Finland and of unsound mind was brought on board by Constable D.H. Horace, B.C. Police at Ucluelet B.C. about 9:00 pm November 25th. They were assigned Stateroom No. 16. On arrival at Port Alberni B.C. at about 3:30 am Nov. 26th, he was found apparently dead by the constable in charge of him. Dr. Hilton, coroner, was summoned and pronounced the man dead by strangulation. The body was landed at Port Alberni in care of B.C. Police. R. Thompson, Master.

Jan. 27 / 1943. While working cargo in No. 2 hold at Zeballos about 1:30 pm, Stephen B. Bubel, seaman, sustained a broken leg. He was landed at Esperanza Hospital and left there in charge of Dr. McLean.

Jan. 14th / 1945. 10:48 pm engines stopped a/c [aircraft] report by two RCAF airmen of seeing man leap overboard. Lifebuoy and light thrown overboard. No.3 lifeboat cleared. Ship maneuvered around lifebuoy endeavoring to pick up man in searchlights.[203]

Another wartime incident of note, reported by Hugh Halliday, appears in an article in the *Legion* magazine of April 25, 1995. "On December 18, 1943, personnel at No. 11 Radio Detachment (Ferrer Point, on the northwest coast of Vancouver Island) saw shells splash close to their unit and reported they were under attack." Panic ensued and aircraft from Coal Harbour and Tofino scrambled to investigate, but only found two small fishing vessels near the area of the reported incident.

Six hours after the reported shelling, the Seattle office of United Press was telephoning Western Air Command headquarters about reports of Vancouver Island being bombed. It was learned that the SS *Princess Maquinna*, passing five miles [8 km] away, had undertaken some 12-pounder gunnery practice, firing toward what the crew took to be an uninhabited shore. The ship's captain claimed his gun crew had only fired two heavy rounds; those on the receiving end claimed there had been anywhere between nine and twenty shell splashes. The presence of a radar site was, of course, a closely guarded secret, apparently even to the *Maquinna*.[204]

In August 1942 Allied forces recaptured the Solomon Islands and began "island hopping" toward Japan. As that campaign progressed, the threat of a Japanese attack on the West Coast slowly dissipated. Nevertheless, people remained vigilant; planes from the various airfields continued their lonely flights out over the Pacific and the "Gumboot Navy" continued patrolling coastal waters. Despite the lessened threat of invasion, the people on the coast, like all Canadians, continued living with the limitations of rationing and blackouts at night. Eventually, the dropping of the atomic bombs on Hiroshima and Nagasaki finally ended the war on August 15, 1945. Shortly afterward, the *Princess Maquinna* sailed to Vancouver to be repainted, returning her to her more familiar peacetime colours.

CHAPTER 19
THE FINAL YEARS

ITH THE WAR years behind her the *Maquinna* continued her faithful service up and down the west coast of Vancouver Island. By 1945 she had been on this route for thirty-two years, and like her sister *Princess* vessels, she was reaching the end of her serviceable life. Six of the *Princess* ships built by Superintendent James Troup in the 1910s and 1920s had been on the water for more than thirty years and, despite regular upkeep, they were becoming decidedly dated. To compound matters further, as the vessels aged, passenger and cargo traffic had slowly declined, due to new roads and new airline services. It became clear that the CPR management faced some serious decisions about its post-war business model. The people of the coast knew the old ship had problems, and many realized the *Maquinna*'s days were numbered, but no one wanted to see her go.

In her many years on the west coast, the *Maquinna* lost a few passengers, several to suicide and some because of medical problems while on board. However, the worst tragedy the vessel ever experienced, in terms of loss of life, occurred near the end of the Good Ship's years on the coast. In January 1949, while the *Maquinna* steamed at night from Nootka to Tahsis, she collided with a smaller vessel. While steering NW-by-W near Bodega Island, the *Maquinna*'s bridge crew sighted a white light off the starboard bow. The helmsman altered course to starboard (the narrow channel did not allow a turn to port) but suddenly the light closed rapidly, forcing him to turn even harder to starboard three more times. At 2:43 a.m., fearing a collision, Captain Peter Leslie ordered the engines full astern. Nonetheless, the *Maquinna* struck the MV *Lorraine* a moment later on the starboard quarter. Leslie ordered the engines stopped while his crew threw lifebuoys to people from the badly damaged *Lorraine*. The *Maquinna*'s crew then lowered No.1 lifeboat, which rescued three people from the side of the *Lorraine*'s gas boat, one of whom was holding onto a gas drum. No more survivors could be found, though the lifeboat continued searching until 4:15 a.m., when the *Maquinna*'s stewardess, Mrs. Joan Leslie, reported that one survivor was suffering from a badly cut arm, and should see a doctor as soon as possible. With the lifeboat back aboard, the ship turned around and proceeded at full speed to the nearby missionary hospital at Esperanza, where the survivors were cared for by Dr. MacLean.

Of the MV *Lorraine*'s seven passengers, four died and three were saved. Why such a small (and seemingly overcrowded) boat as the MV *Lorraine* was on the water at that time of night is unknown. The *Maquinna* and her crew were not held responsible for the accident.

Later that year, a tragic incident occurred in far-off Toronto Harbour that had a considerable impact on the *Princess Maquinna* and other BC passenger ships. At 2:30 a.m. on September 16, 1949, a fire erupted aboard the passenger ship SS *Noronic* as she lay tied up to a dock in Toronto's harbour. The ship regularly plied the Great Lakes as a tourist ship and her passengers were asleep on board. The fire claimed the lives of 118 passengers, most of them Americans. An inquiry recommended stricter fire regulations be imposed on all Canadian passenger ships. The cost of implementing these new regulations put such a financial burden on Canadian shipping companies, including the Union Steamship Co. and the CPR in BC, that many companies chose to tie up their older ships rather than spend the money needed to meet the new regulations.

By 1952 the CPR head office took a long, hard look at its west coast route, assessing every aspect of the service in an attempt to decide what to do with the nearly forty-year-old *Maquinna*. As an immediate priority, the managers decided to assess the state of the ship's thirty-nine-year-old boilers, suspecting they needed repairing or replacing. However, even before the inspection, a CPR official declared that "due to her advanced age it is not considered that it would be economically sound, or justified, to spend large sums of money on this ship."[205]

The CPR also looked closely at the passenger and cargo numbers, reporting that "the *Maquinna's* holds were on average only one quarter full; except during the summer tourist season, only 30 percent of her berths were booked. It was estimated that Queen Charlotte Airways were carrying 85 percent of the West Coast passenger traffic."[206] A flight on QCA from Vancouver to Tofino cost $21 and took forty-five minutes. In comparison the fare on the *Princess Maquinna* cost $19.45 and took two days.[207]

As for the declining freight statistics, the CPR noted that "Within recent years several fish packing operations have placed their own vessels in service on the west coast and many canneries have transferred their operations to Steveston—on the mainland at the mouth of the Fraser River—in order to centralize their activities. Fish boats, after unloading their product, are loading groceries, equipment, etc. for northbound voyages to their own establishments on the West Coast."[208] This new strategy by the fish-packing companies severely cut into the CPR's bottom line on its west coast route.

Unquestionably, the continuing development of roads to various coastal communities also impinged on the business. In 1946 the new road from Port Hardy to Coal Harbour in Quatsino Sound had already forced the CPR to curtail service on the northern leg of the *Maquinna's* ten-day run up the coast. In 1952 a reasonably good road had been established from Victoria to Shawnigan Lake over the Malahat, and by using connecting logging roads trucks could now transport groceries to Port Renfrew, further cutting into CPR revenues. With the potential of other roads being built, perhaps to Bamfield, Ucluelet and Tofino, the CPR realized that more roads would make "a steamship service on the West Coast extremely unprofitable."[209]

Each year the CPR received an annual subsidy from the federal government to maintain the west coast service. In 1952 that amounted to $161,792. In an attempt to stave off the inevitable, the company made hopeful overtures to the appropriate ministry to see if that figure could be increased in order to continue the west coast service. The government, however, refused to increase the subsidy.

Cockroaches added to these woes. In the late 1940s and into the 1950s these unwelcome passengers infested the *Maquinna*. They appeared everywhere and hid in the dark recesses of the ship, prompting the ship's stewards to devise unique ways of catching them. One of their most successful methods involved filling a glass tumbler with a little water and greasing the inside of the tumbler with some butter. The cockroaches climbed into the tumbler but the slippery butter prevented them from climbing out again. Soon they exhausted themselves in their attempts to escape, and drowned. The stewards emptied the tumblers each morning but some passengers "arose repeatedly in the night to empty the water tumbler and its victims out the porthole."[210] Since the cockroaches liked dark environs, regular passengers knew to lift the bedsheets and carry out an inspection of their bunks before bedding down. If they found some of the creatures they could call a steward to remove them.

Against this background of woes, the CPR announced that it would withdraw the *Maquinna* from service on Wednesday, September 24, 1952, to carry out a full inspection of her boilers, with no indication of how long the ship would be out of service. Her final trip before this inspection was slated to depart from Victoria on Thursday, September 18.

An article in the *Vancouver Sun* on Tuesday, August 10, 1952, quoted a CPR official as saying:

> The situation is that the vessel is old and her boilers have seen good service. But the cost of overhauling her and making her good as

This cartoon appeared in the Vancouver *Province* on August 25, 1952, following the announcement by the CPSOS that the *Princess Maquinna*'s boilers were in poor shape, but before the *Maquinna* made her final trip. IMAGE COURTESY OF THE VANCOUVER *PROVINCE*.

new again might cost more than the trade at present warrants. The cost of putting a better ship on this route would also not pay. West Coast trade has changed radically over the past years. The cargo there used to be paper, fish, timber and other big parcels, out and home. Now there is just a little to cover her bottom line only and you can safely say the ship is running at a loss. The *Maquinna* was formerly a good passenger ship. Everybody using the West Coast traveled in her. Now mostly they fly. You can't pay the way of an empty ship. She is a magnificent tradition but unfortunately there is no money in tradition.[211]

Even if the *Maquinna*'s boilers could be repaired inexpensively, management realized that she was living on borrowed time and proposed three options for when she ended her career. They could abandon the west coast route altogether; replace the *Maquinna* with the *Princess Norah* on a permanent basis; or acquire a smaller vessel to replace the *Maquinna*.

The announcement of the *Maquinna*'s imminent withdrawal from service prompted a flurry of responses from a variety of municipal, provincial and federal spokesmen. The Honorable Robert Mayhew, Minister of Fisheries, stated that he would support the building of roads to the west coast. "Money would be better spent on permanent roads rather than on annual shipping subsidies,"[212] he told the *Daily Colonist*. Anticipating the loss of the *Maquinna*, Esquimalt MLA Frank Matthews wired Union Steamships asking it to take over the run left vacant if the *Maquinna* failed to pass her boiler test. Port Alberni put forward the idea that it would make a much better terminus for a new service than Victoria, saying this would cut a couple of days off the schedule. Clo-oose residents resubmitted their plan presented to the provincial government some twenty years earlier, asking for a road to be built to their community, and Tofino's president of the Chamber of Commerce, Tom Gibson, declared Tofino had been promised a road for fifty years and "now was the time to get on with it."[213] He added that a road would cost about $1 million and would be paid for in ten years, given that the CPR received a subsidy of over $100,000 a year to run the service. "The whole economy of the West Coast is at stake," said Mr. R. Barr, a member of the Tofino Board of Trade. "We are facing an intolerable situation. We must have steamship or highway connections in order to survive."[214] It would be another seven years before a rough gravel road finally opened in 1959 connecting Tofino with Port Alberni.

Although her final trip was scheduled for September 18, 1952, the good ship *Maquinna*'s final trip up the west coast actually occurred some weeks earlier. She left Victoria on August 26 and safely arrived at Chamiss Bay in Kyuquot Sound (which by then had become her northern terminus) on August 29. She departed on the same day, disembarked forty-two children returning to school at Kakawis, loaded six tons of fish at Clayoquot, held an emergency boat drill at Port Alberni, and arrived back in Victoria at 6:33 p.m. on August 31. She then proceeded to Vancouver via the Gulf Islands, arriving at 6:30 p.m. She departed Vancouver at 3:50 p.m. on September 2 and arrived back in Victoria at 3:20 a.m. September 3. A very routine and uneventful trip.

On September 4, with forty passengers and cargo loaded for what was intended to be her second-to-last trip, "Old Faithful" cast off from the Belleville Street wharf at 12:17 a.m. However, a few minutes after leaving the dock her boilers gave out and could no longer produce enough power to drive the ship; she managed to limp only as far as the nearby BA Oil dock. The final entry in her log reads: "Sep 4 / 52. Arr. 12:50 BA Oil Dock. Port Landing."

Captain Carthew assembled those passengers who had not retired for the night and informed them that the trip was cancelled. He told them that they were welcome to stay on board overnight and they would be served breakfast in the morning, but that they then must find their own way up the coast as best they could. The next day the crew unloaded the ship's cargo and stored it in the CPR freight sheds, pending arrangements to send it up the coast. The mail was returned to the Vancouver Post Office, where officials began exploring ways to deliver it.

While most west coast communities could find ways to survive without the *Maquinna* on a short-term basis, isolated places like Kyuquot keenly felt the loss of "Old Faithful." To bring in essential food supplies, the village arranged for fish company packer boats to carry in what they needed.

By the end of September, as a stop-gap measure, the CPR chartered the thousand-ton SS *Chilliwack* from Frank Waterhouse Ltd.—a subsidiary of Union Steamships—to make a one-off emergency run carrying the *Maquinna*'s freight from her final voyage to coastal communities. The *Veta C*, another Waterhouse vessel, took over for the remainder of the winter. (The *Norah* was needed on other routes and so wasn't available to fill in.) The *Veta C* provided no passenger accommodation and carried only freight, so the CPR continued looking for an adequate vessel that could take passengers as well as freight, thus filling the role of the *Maquinna*. In the years following, the small and ugly *Princess of Alberni*, the *Northland Prince* and the *Tahsis Prince* all filled in while folk on the west coast waited for the *Maquinna* to be repaired, or for roads to be built. Increasingly, passengers wanting to leave the west coast chose to make their way to Ucluelet and take the *Uchuck*, which sailed three times a week to Port Alberni, from where they would continue by road.

After a brief inspection of the *Maquinna*'s boilers, CPR management decided that repairs would not be undertaken. She remained tied up at the BA Oil dock until the spring of 1953, when she was sold to the Union Steamship Company and towed to Victoria Machinery Depot, where her superstructure and interior fittings were removed and sold off. Ivan Clarke of Hot Springs Cove purchased the stateroom keys. In April 1953 Captain J.O. Williams, manager of BC Coastal Steamships, a subsidiary of the CPR, presented the *Maquinna*'s bell to the jovial, pipe-smoking Rev. John Leighton, once the minister at St. Columba's church in Tofino. He wanted it to call

The *Princess Maquinna*'s binnacle was donated to the Ucluelet
Sea Cadets when she was scrapped. It now resides with the
Ucluelet and Area Historical Society. CLAUDIA COLE PHOTO.

The *Princess Maquinna* ended her life as an ore barge, the *Taku*, carrying ore from Alaska to a smelter in Tacoma, Washington. In 1962 she was finally broken up for scrap, ending her long career. JACK LINDSAY PHOTO. IMAGE CVA 374-126 COURTESY OF THE CITY OF VANCOUVER ARCHIVES.

patrons to services at the Mission for Seamen in Vancouver where he then served. Several former *Maquinna* skippers attended the ceremony: R.W. Carthew, S.G. Hunter, P.L. Leslie, L.W. McDonald and Martin MacKinnon. At the same event, Williams presented the *Maquinna*'s binnacle, which held the ship's compass on the bridge, to the Ucluelet Sea Cadets.

Captain Williams also ensured that the Bullen family received the *Maquinna*'s nameplate; the Bullen shipyard in Esquimalt had built the ship, forty years earlier. In a letter of thanks to Williams, J.W.F.

Bullen wrote: "I proffer my most sincere and heartfelt thanks to you for making it possible to possess this memory of the old ship." Also attending the ceremony was 17-year-old Melville Palmer, who had been born aboard the ship on April 18, 1936, when his mother was travelling south from Jeune Landing.

Later, a tug towed the *Maquinna* to Vancouver, where her engines and boilers were removed and her hull became an ore-carrying barge, renamed *Taku*. The name honoured the Alaskan inlet where her cargo would be loaded. Stripped down and with a modern steel crane installed, she joined four other ore carriers owned by Straits Towing, each carrying 2,000-ton loads of concentrated copper-lead-zinc ore from Taku to the smelter at Tacoma. The ore came from the Tulsequah mine in northern BC near the junction of the Tulsequah and Taku Rivers, having been transported some 30 miles (50 km) down to Taku Inlet on river barges. The sea-going barges off-loaded the ore from the river barges using their own cranes. Sometimes the *Taku* also collected ore at the mine at Britannia Beach on Howe Sound and took it to Tacoma.

The *Taku* continued this heavy and unglamorous work until 1962, when Acme Machinery Ltd. in False Creek, Vancouver, broke her up for scrap. An ignominious end for one of the best-loved ships in BC history.

CHAPTER 20

TRIBUTES

ESTCOASTERS IN the many outposts served by the *Maquinna* felt betrayed by the CPR. Some argued that the company had deliberately allowed the ship to deteriorate in order to remove her from service. Most had grown so attached to the *Maquinna* they found it extremely difficult to acknowledge the changing times and many problems that inevitably led to the ship's demise.

While other *Princess* ships also held special places in the hearts of those who travelled in BC waters, none held such deep connections to her passengers as the *Princess Maquinna*. The people living on the west coast of Vancouver Island relied on and loved that vessel, and a special bond had built up for nearly forty years. They became friends with its captains and crew members, treating them as extended family members—the *Princess Maquinna* was "their" boat. James K. Nesbitt wrote this eulogy to the ship in the *Daily Colonist* in 1953:

> The *Princess Maquinna* became an institution along the rugged, splendid West Coast, she poked her nose against rickety docks, and tied up alongside floating logging camps, and often anchored out to unload her freight by tender, or into Indian dugouts. Those who travelled in her will never forget her—the strange zig-zag passage-ways, the unpretentious, homey lounge, the tiny smoking rooms, the cozy dining saloon with its atmosphere of a kindly home. There

were many who could never resist a *Maquinna* trip each year. They learned to love the vessel, to feel safe in her. Most of them liked to be in her, too, when there was a storm, and they gathered round the warm funnel, as the ship rolled and plunged, the salt sea spray in their faces, the wind whistling in the rigging, the boards groaning and creaking.[215]

When the *Princess Maquinna* ended her service on the west coast, the chorus of protests swelled, and then gradually faded as the coastal communities adjusted to the new reality. Meanwhile, writers and journalists familiar with the ship outdid themselves writing articles commemorating her.

In her book *Personality Ships of British Columbia*, Ruth Greene quotes journalist Cecil Maiden's wry and fond tribute to the *Maquinna*:

The *Maquinna* is an ugly ship. With her thin, elongated funnel and her ill-proportioned bow, she is ugly from any direction in which you look at her. She is also one of the most uncomfortable vessels on which I have ever travelled—with one green-leathered unlovely public room to sit in, and a couple of padded benches along a central space adjoining the purser's office. But like the Ugly Duckling of the fairy tale, she has stolen the hearts of the people, and I doubt if any vessel afloat could be more beloved.[216]

Greene continues, sharing her own knowledge of the ship:

And that is just about how the West Coast thinks of her, for she is not just a part of their history; she has made it ... At times when no fish boat could fight through the wild seas ... always around the headland or behind the driving rain, has been the *Maquinna*— *nearly* always on schedule; nearly always with a handful of people coming to build a new home, or her ruminating Indians on their way from the market to their ancestral fish grounds ... She has deepened the bonds of family and opened up the solitary places.[217]

Perhaps no one put it better than Dorothy Abraham in her book *Lone Cone*, a memoir of her years living on Vargas Island and in Tofino:

> There was always excitement on boat days, and everyone went down to see the *Princess Maquinna* come in and to pick up their stores and mail. They came from up the inlets, from over the mountains, through the forests. They rode horseback or they walked from miles inland. They came in dugouts, row-boats, put-puts and all manner of craft. Indians would paddle out to welcome the *Maquinna,* wearing gay colours, gracious in their canoes. As she bustled in and out of 26 ports of call, she became a friend to all—their link with civilization. If ever a ship took on body and soul and personality, lived fully, loved by all who sailed in her, it was *Princess Maquinna.* And there's a catch in the throats of those who loved her to know that now it's farewell forever.[218]

In 1958, a few years after the demise of the *Princess Maquinna,* the CPR sold the *Princess Norah* to Northland Navigation, which renamed her the *Canadian Prince.* In 1964 she was stripped of her machinery and towed to Kodiak, Alaska, where she became the Beachcomber restaurant and dance hall. With her sale the CPR ended more than half a century of freight and passenger service to the small coastal communities of Vancouver Island. Robert Turner states in his book *Pacific Princesses* that: "While the CPR's retirement from the steamship business had been rapid in the 1950s, in the early 1960s it was precipitous."[219]

The last *Princess* ship, the *Princess of Vancouver,* entered service in 1955 carrying passengers and automobiles between Vancouver and Nanaimo. However, following an eight-month-long shipping strike in 1958, the BC government purchased the BC routes of the Black Ball Ferry Line, and then created the BC Ferries Corporation. The combined effect of the strike and the creation of BC Ferries served as the death knell for the remaining CPR coastal service, which slowly began to dissipate. In February 1959 the last night boats that had sailed to and from Vancouver and Victoria for decades made their final journeys. The next year the CPR found it could no longer compete with BC Ferries, which ran eight return-trip sailings a day between Tsawwassen and Swartz Bay, leaving the *Princess of Vancouver* on the Nanaimo route as the sole CPR *Princess* ship still sailing on the Pacific coast. Slowly the CPR sold off the old *Princess* ships, while others in its fleet continued to carry freight and rail cars. On November 17, 1998, however, Seaspan Coastal Intermodal Company bought what remained of the Canadian Pacific's coastal marine operations, ending an era of shipping in BC waters that had served so many British Columbians so well for over a century.

Though no CPR ships ply BC waters today, those wishing to take a trip like the one travellers took on the *Princess Maquinna* in 1924 do have some options. They can board the *Uchuck III*, based in Gold River, on a variety of day trips to Nootka and Zeballos and an overnight trip to Kyuquot; or the *Lady Barkley* from Port Alberni on day cruises down Alberni Inlet to Bamfield. From Campbell River, the Marine Link's MV *Aurora Explorer* provides a limited number of passengers a five-day trip north up Seymour Narrows and into the inlets of the Broughton Archipelago. They all perform the same kind of passenger/freight service once carried out by the *Maquinna*. Those wanting to take a longer sea journey can pay thousands of dollars to travel on foreign-owned cruise ships from Vancouver to Alaska. None, however, can replicate the memorable experience those hypothetical 1924 passengers enjoyed for only $39 for a week-long trip along the west coast of Vancouver Island aboard the *Princess Maquinna*.

The Belleville Street terminal in Victoria, where the *Princess Maquinna* once sailed to and from, still serves as a shipping terminal for the Black Ball's MV *Coho*, which makes twice-daily voyages across the Strait of Juan de Fuca to Port Angeles on Washington State's Olympic Peninsula. Few physical reminders of the *Princess Maquinna* still exist, save for her bell and binnacle, fittingly housed at Tofino and Ucluelet respectively. Her legend still survives in the annals of British Columbia's maritime history, where the *Princess Maquinna* is lovingly remembered as the "Best-Loved Boat" that ever sailed the waters of British Columbia.

A *Princess Maquinna* pennant from Ken Gibson's personal collection.
MARK KAARREMAA PHOTO.

ACKNOWLEDGEMENTS

M Y THANKS TO Margaret Horsfield for her help with this book. The research material she provided proved invaluable, as were her editing skills.

Thanks also to Captain David Young, author and former skipper of the *Uchuck lll,* and Captain Mal Walsh, former deep sea tug master, for helping me understand how to navigate in fog, how triple expansion engines work and generally answering any query I had about things nautical.

My gratitude to Leona Taylor who, over many years, scoured Victoria newspapers in the BC archives, and created digital files itemizing thousands of articles. These proved an invaluable resource.

I would also like to acknowledge Gwen Hansen of the Quatsino Archives Association; Heather Cooper of the Bamfield Historical Society; Peter Timmermans, Claudia Cole and other volunteers at the Ucluelet and Area Historical Society and Brenda McCorquodale for her articles about Northern Vancouver Island on her web site *Undiscovered Coast.* Nancy Lyon enlightened me on the early history of Clo-oose by allowing me to see letters and photos relating to the lives of her grandparents there in the early 1920s.

I also wish to thank the late Bob Wingen of Tofino and Margaret Thompson of Ucluelet for allowing me to interview them and providing me first hand knowledge of the *Maquinna.*

CPR *Princess* ship expert Robert D. Bob Turner generously shared information and photographs and Lois and Barry Warner provide me photographs taken by her father Harold Monks. Dal Matterson provided photos of his parents' "tour bus" on Long Beach. Victoria's Tessa Bousfield and Denton Pendergast helped me find one particularly evasive picture. I am grateful to them for their efforts on my behalf, as I am to Marc Phillips for his extraordinary photo shopping skills, transforming old photographs into gems. Jason Hummel provided me with his pictures of the West Coast Trail and John MacFarlane of *Nauticapedia*.ca offered help and sage advice on a number of issues.

Thank you all.

NOTES

Chapter 1

1 Phillips, 111.

2 Henry, 96.

3 *Daily Colonist,* November 2, 1913.

4 Francis, 67.

5 Horsfield 2008, 215.

6 Greene, 165.

7 *Daily Colonist,* January 12, 1901.

8 Hacking and Lamb, 186.

9 Turner 1984, 120.

10 Hacking and Lamb, 193-4.

Chapter 2

11 Earl Marsh Collection, Box 8, "History," call number 937330-0008. #5818.

12 Hacking and Lamb, 232.

13 *Daily Colonist,* December 21, 1912.

14 Earl Marsh Collection, Box 8, "History." Letter from Troup to George Bury VP and Gen Manager of CPR in Winnipeg.

15 *Daily Colonist,* September 6, 1912.

16 *Daily Colonist,* May 6, 1913.

17 Robertson, 7.

18 Earl Marsh Collection, Box 7, "Saints and Sinners," call number 937330-0007. Troup, James. Letter to Bullen's, July 14, 1913.

19 Earl Marsh Collection, Box 7, "Saints and Sinners," call number 937330-0007. #5817.

20 Earl Marsh Collection, Box 7, "Saints and Sinners," call number 937330-0007. Troup, James. Letter to H.W. Brodie, July 31, 1913.

21 Earl Marsh Collection, Box 7, "Saints and Sinners," call number 937330-0007. Troup, James. Thursday Report, July 31, 1913.

22 Earl Marsh Collection, Box 7, "Saints and Sinners," call number 937330-0007. CPR Report on SS Princess Maquinna Maiden Voyage.

23 Earl Marsh Collection, Box 7, "Saints and Sinners," call number 937330-0007. CPR Report on SS Princess Maquinna Maiden Voyage.

24 Earl Marsh Collection, Box 7, "Saints and Sinners," call number 937330-0007. CPR Report on SS Princess Maquinna Maiden Voyage.

25 Earl Marsh Collection, Box 7, "Saints and Sinners," call number 937330-0007. CPR Report on SS Princess Maquinna Maiden Voyage.

26 Earl Marsh Collection, Box 7, "Saints and Sinners," call number 937330-0007. Troup, James. Thursday Report, July 31, 1913.

27 Earl Marsh Collection, Box 7, "Saints and Sinners," call number 937330-0007. Troup, James. Letter to B.C. Marine Railway Company Ltd., July 28, 1913.

28 Horsfield 2008, 215.

29 Hacking and Lamb, 151.

30 Mike Hamilton, personal papers.

31 Horsfield 2008, 216.

32 *Daily Colonist*, February 26, 1914.

33 *Daily Colonist*, March 24, 1914.

34 *Daily Colonist*, November 13, 1913.

Chapter 3

35 Brodie.

36 Anthony Guppy, 11.

37 Halkett.

38 Horsfield 2016, 3.

39 Horsfield 2016, 3.

40 Scott 1974, 35.

41 Anthony Guppy, 11.

Chapter 4

42 Neitzel, 8.

43 Rogers, 77.

44 Rogers, 78.

45 Neitzel, 21.

46 *Daily Colonist*, June 13, 1907

Chapter 5

47 Scott 1974, 38.

48 West Coast Development Co.

49 West Coast Development Co.

50 Newitt.

51 Pearson.

52 Scott 1974, 46.

53 Paterson and Basque, 138.

54 Scott 1974, 47.

55 Newitt.

56 Scott 1974, 47.

57 Scott 1986, 20.

58 Paterson and Basque, 144.

59 Nicholson, 286–7.

60 Wells, 15.

Chapter 6

61 Nicholson, 150–1.

62 Scott 1974, 85–6.

63 Nicholson, 155.

64 Nicholson, 154.

65 Bob Wingen interview with author, July 28, 2016.

66 Horsfield 2008, 224.

67 Peterson 1999, 238.

68 *Daily Colonist*, December 30, 1931.

69 *Daily Colonist*, December 19, 1976.

70 Bob Wingen interview with author, July 28, 2016.

71 Sivertz, Gus. *Victoria Times*, November 23, 1957, 4.

72 Scott 1986, 20.

Chapter 7

73 Peterson 1999, 32.

74 Scott 1994, 25.

75 Scott 1994, 88–9.

76 Phillips, 112

77 George Johnson, 441.

78 Scott 1994, 27.

79 Peterson 1999, 235.

80 Scott 1986, 21–2.

81 Scott 1986, 42.

82 Peterson 1999, 24.

Chapter 8

83 Mike Hamilton, personal papers.

84 Horsfield and Kennedy, 175.

85 Nicholson, 245.

86 Earl Marsh Collection, Box 8, "History," call number 937330-0008. Marsh, Earl. *The West Coast of Vancouver Island.*

87 Phillips, 155.

88 Earl Marsh Collection, Box 22, call number 937330-0008. CPR Schedule June July and August, 1930.

89 Anthony Guppy, 10.

90 Lillard, 217.

91 Lillard, 223.

92 Earl Marsh Collection, Box 22, call number 937330-0008. High Court of Justice Judgment. Wednesday October 10, 1934.

93   Bloom, 11.

94   Phillips, 111.

Chapter 9

95   Peterson 1999, 118.

96   Horsfield and Kennedy, 179-80.

97   Bloom.

98   *Westerly News*, July 2, 2014.

99   Phillips, 152.

100   Horsfield 2008, 219.

Chapter 10

101   *Daily Colonist*, November 28, 1915.

102   *Daily Colonist*, November 28, 1915.

103   *Daily Colonist*, November 28, 1915.

104   Paterson.

105   *Daily Colonist*, November 28, 1915.

106   *Daily Colonist*, December 12, 1976.

107   Bloom.

108   Stark, 216.

109   Ron MacLeod, private papers.

110   Ron MacLeod, private papers.

111   Bob Wingen interview with author, July 28, 2016.

112   Bob Wingen interview with author, July 28, 2016.

113   Phillips, 111.

114   Ken Gibson interview with author, November 8, 2012.

115   Young, 71.

116   Robertson.

Chapter 11

117   Moore, June 1977.

118   Horsfield and Kennedy, 321.

119   Robertson.

120 Horsfield and Kennedy, 274.

121 Moser, 369.

122 Moser, 445.

123 Horsfield and Kennedy, 362. Testimony presented at the Truth and Reconciliation Commission's Port Alberni hearings, April 13, 2012.

124 Earl Marsh Collection, Box 13, call number 937330-0013.

125 Earl Marsh Collection, Box 13, call number 937330-0013.

126 Earl Marsh Collection, Box 13, call number 937330-0013.

127 Moore, June 1977.

128 Moser.

129 Hogg, 85.

130 Turner 2001.

131 Brodie.

132 Gibson, 33–4.

133 Gibson, 53.

134 Gibson, 42.

135 Gibson, 75–6.

136 Bloom.

137 Horsfield and Kennedy, 187.

Chapter 12

138 Kaehn, 40.

139 Horsfield and Kennedy, 89.

140 *British Colonist*, March 16, 1869.

141 Leadem, 115.

Chapter 13

142 Horsfield and Kennedy, 44.

143 Brodie.

144 Brodie.

145 Abraham, 73.

146 Sage.

147 Moore, March 1977.

148   Bloom.

149   Bloom.

150   Bloom.

151   Bloom.

Chapter 14

152   Walter Guppy, 35-6.

153   "Old Timer," 5.

154   Skinner.

155   Skinner.

156   Skinner.

157   Skinner.

158   Skinner.

159   Skinner.

160   Skinner.

161   Young, 223.

162   Brodie.

163   *Daily Colonist*, December 5, 1911.

164   *Daily Colonist*, December 5, 1911.

165   *Daily Colonist*, December 3, 1911.

166   *Daily Colonist*, March 9, 1919.

Chapter 15

167   Johnson and Walls, 193.

168   Grant, 16-17.

169   Moore, June 1977.

170   Ildstad.

171   Moore, June 1977.

172   Maiden.

173   Maiden.

174   Smith, 19.

175   Tamm, 119.

Chapter 16

176 Brodie.

177 Tamm, 120-1.

178 Turner, 2001, 46.

179 *Victoria Daily Times*, May 30, 1970.

180 Horsfield 2008, 221-2, quoting Boyce.

181 "Old Timer," 5.

182 Horsfield 2008, 221-2.

183 Tyson, Ian. "Summer Wages," from the album *Cowboyography*, 1987.

Chapter 17

184 Brodie.

185 Hacking and Lamb, 267.

186 Nesbitt 1975, 2.

187 Anthony Guppy, 13.

188 "Old Timer," 5.

189 Horsfield 2008, 222.

190 "Old Timer," 5.

191 Earl Marsh Collection, Box 7, "Saints and Sinners," call number 937330-0007. March 1938, 2.

192 *Daily Colonist*, March 25, 1925.

193 Henry, 105.

194 Margaret Horsfield interview with Margaret Warren, June 23, 1996.

195 Phillips, 81.

196 Young, 53.

Chapter 18

197 Peterson, 1991.

198 Bossin, 61

199 McLeod.

200 Robertson, 75-6.

201 Robertson, 394.

202   Robertson, 75–6.

203   Robertson, 71-2.

204   Halliday.

Chapter 19

205   Earl Marsh Collection CPR letter, September 3, 1952. Accession File 100,128.

206   Hacking and Lamb, 300.

207   Earl Marsh Collection CPR letter, September 3, 1952. Accession File 100,128.

208   Earl Marsh Collection CPR letter, September 3, 1952. Accession File 100,128.

209   Earl Marsh Collection CPR letter, September 3, 1952. Accession File 100,128.

210   Horsfield and Kennedy, 431-2.

211   *Vancouver Sun*, August 10, 1952.

212   *Daily Colonist,* August 23, 1952.

213   *Daily Colonist,* August 21, 1952.

214   *Daily Colonist,* August 21, 1952.

Chapter 20

215   Nesbitt 1953.

216   Greene, 212.

217   Greene, 212.

218   Nesbitt 1953.

219   Turner 1977, 220.

BIBLIOGRAPHY

Abraham, Dorothy. *Lone Cone: Life on the West Coast of Vancouver Island.* Victoria: self-published, 1945.

Bloom, A. "The Fabulous West Coast," *Raincoast Chronicles* 11 (1987), 10–15.

Bossin, Bob. *Settling Clayoquot.* Victoria: Sound Heritage Series #33, 1981.

Boyce, W.J. "Navigating Steamers in Fog on the BC Coast," *Canadian Merchant Service Guild Annual*, 1923.

Brodie, H. *General Passenger Agent Inspection Trip, Steamship Service: West Coast of Vancouver Island, Steamship Princess Maquinna.* 1918. Vancouver: Wally Chung Collection, UBC Special Collections, call number CC_TX_285_012. https://open.library.ubc.ca/collections/chung/chungtext/items/1.0354852.

Earl Marsh Collection. Series MS-3254: Scrapbooks, Canadian Pacific Railway Company records, and subject files. Victoria: BC Archives. https://search-bcarchives.royalbcmuseum.bc.ca/scrapbooks-canadi-an-pacific-railway-company-records-and-subject-files.

Francis, Daniel (ed.). *Encyclopedia of British Columbia.* Madeira Park: Harbour Publishing, 2000.

Gibson, Gordon, with Carol Renison. *Bull of the Woods: The Gordon Gibson Story.* Vancouver: Douglas and McIntyre, 1980.

Grant, Peter. *Wish You Were Here: Life on Vancouver Island in Historical Photographs.* Victoria: TouchWood Editions, 2002.

Greene, Ruth. *Personality Ships of British Columbia.* West Vancouver: Marine Tapestry Publications, 1969.

Guppy, Anthony. *Tofino Kid*. Duncan: Firgrove Publishing, 2000.

Guppy, Walter. *Wet Coast Ventures: Mine-Finding on Vancouver Island*. Victoria: Cappis Press, 1988.

Hacking, Norman R., and Lamb, W. Kaye. *The Princess Story: A Century and a Half of West Coast Shipping*. Vancouver: Mitchell Press, 1974.

Hagelund, W.A. *Whalers No More*. Madeira Park: Harbour Publishing, 1987.

Halkett, H.D. "The Good Ship Maquinna," *Daily Colonist*, May 18, 1980, *The Islander* supplement, 10-11. https://archive.org/details/dailycolonist19800518/page/n75/mode/2up.

Halliday, Hugh. "Winding Down Western Air Command: Air Force, Part 32," *Legion*, April 25, 2009. https://legionmagazine.com/en/winding-down-western-air-command-air-force-part-32/.

Hancock, Eleanor. *Salt Chuck Stories from Vancouver Island's West Coast: Zeballos, Nootka Sound, Kyuquot*. Kamloops: Partners in Publishing, 2006.

Hempsall, Leslie. *We Stand On Guard for Thee: A History of the War Years at the Royal Canadian Air Force Stations, Ucluelet and Tofino*. Surrey: Coomber-Hampsall Publishing, 2003.

Henry, Tom. *Westcoasters: Boats that Built British Columbia*. Madeira Park: Harbour Publishing, 1998.

Hogg, Robert. "Evaluating historic fertility change in small reserve populations," *BC Studies* 101, (Spring 1994), 79-95. https://ojs.library.ubc.ca/index.php/bcstudies/article/view/868.

Horsfield, Margaret. "The Enduring Legacy of Josephine Tilden." *Hakai Magazine*, June 2016.

Horsfield, Margaret. *Voices From the Sound*. Nanaimo: Salal Books, 2008.

Horsfield, Margaret, and Kennedy, Ian. *Tofino and Clayoquot Sound: A History*. Madeira Park: Harbour Publishing, 2014.

Ildstad, I.M. "West Coast Ships," *Daily Colonist*, April 13, 1980, *The Islander* supplement, 16. https://archive.org/details/dailycolonist19800413/page/n85/mode/2up.

Johnson, George (ed.). *The All Red Line: The Annals and Aims of the Pacific Cable Project*. Ottawa: James Hope and Sons, 1903.

Johnson, Louise. *Not Without Hope*. Matsqui: Maple Lane Publishing, 1992.

Johnson, Peter. *Glyphs and Gallows: The Rock Art of Clo-oose and the Wreck of the John Bright.* Surrey: Heritage House, 1999.

Johnson, Peter, and Walls, John. *To the Lighthouse: An Explorer's Guide to the Island Lighthouses of Southwestern BC.* Victoria: Heritage House, 2015.

Kaehn, Michael. *The Hot Springs Cove Story: The Beginnings of the Maquinna Marine Provincial Park.* Madeira Park: Harbour Publishing, 2019.

Leadem, Tim. *Hiking the West Coast of Vancouver Island.* Vancouver: Greystone Books, 2008.

Lillard, Charles. *Seven Shillings a Year: The History of Vancouver Island.* Ganges: Horsdal and Schubart, 1986.

McLeod, Islay. "When Time Stopped," *The Sound,* November 30, 1990, reprinted in Brubacher, J., and Cunningham, C., *The Sound Anthology: News Around Clayoquot Sound.* Tofino: *The Sound,* 1997.

Macy, Harold. *San Josef.* New Westminster: Tidewater Press, 2019.

Maiden, Cecil. "The Man in the Tropical Trees," ("The Other Side of the Island," No. 4), *Victoria Daily Times,* December 2, 1950, magazine section.

Moore, Bill. "The 'Good Ship Maquinna,'" *BC Lumberman,* June 1977, 46-9. http://www.wdmoore.ca/articles/082%20June%2077.htm.

Moore, Bill. "The Gyppo," *BC Lumberman,* March 1977, 56-7. http://www.wdmoore.ca/articles/079%20Mar%2077.htm.

Moser, Father Charles. *Reminiscences of the West Coast of Vancouver Island.* Victoria: Acme Press, 1926.

Neitzel, Michael C. *The Valencia Tragedy.* Surrey: Heritage House, 1995.

Nesbitt, James K. "Memories of *Maquinna* Fill West Coast Annals," *Daily Colonist,* March 1, 1953, 7. https://archive.org/details/dailycolonist0353uvic/page/n7/mode/2up.

Nesbitt, James K. "*Princess Norah*'s Maiden Voyage Like Miniature Ocean Cruise," *Daily Colonist,* August 31, 1975, *The Islander* supplement, 2-3. https://archive.org/details/dailycolonist19750831/page/n57/mode/2up

Newitt, Angela. "Some Childhood Memories of Clo'oose," *Raincoast Chronicles* 11 (1987), 16-24.

Nicholson, George. *Vancouver Island's West Coast.* Victoria: George Nicholson, 1965.

"Old Timer." "Ships and Sailors on West Coast of Island: 'Old Timer' Tells of Little Ships and Giant Sailors from the Early Days to the Present times," *West Coast Advocate*, July 7, 1955, 5.

Paterson T.W. "Raging Storm Claimed Last Square-Rigger," *Daily Colonist*, December 19, 1965, *The Islander* supplement, 10-11. https://archive.org/details/dailycolonist19651219/page/n63/mode/2up.

Paterson, T., and Basque, Garnet. *Ghost Towns and Mining Camps of Vancouver Island*. Nanoose Bay: Heritage House, 2000.

Pearson, John. *Surrey-Delta Messenger*, October 24, 1974.

Peterson, Jan. *Journeys: Down the Alberni Canal to Barkley Sound*. Lantzville: Oolican Books, 1999.

Peterson, Jan. "Minutes of the Feb. 13, 1991 meeting of the Alberni Historical Society," *Alberni Valley Times*, "Valley in Review," February 14, 1991.

Phillips, Judith. *Our Whole Bamfield Saga: Pioneer Life on Vancouver Island's West Coast*. Self-published, 2015.

Robertson, Neil. *The Good Ship Maquinna*. n.p.: self-published, 2000.

Rogers, Ted. *Shipwrecks of British Columbia*. Vancouver: J.J. Douglas, 1973.

Sage, H.N. "The Mecca of Friendly Cove," *Second Annual Report and Proceedings of the BC Historical Association*, 1924.

Scott, R. Bruce. *Bamfield Years: Recollections*. Victoria: Sono Nis, 1986.

Scott, R. Bruce. *Barkley Sound: A History of the Pacific Rim National Park Area*. Victoria: self-published, 1972.

Scott, R. Bruce. *"Breakers Ahead!"* Sidney: Review Publishing, 1970.

Scott, R. Bruce. *Gentleman on Imperial Service: A Story of the Trans-Pacific Telecommunications Cable*. Victoria: Sono Nis, 1994.

Scott, R. Bruce. *People of the Southwest Coast of Vancouver Island*. Victoria: self-published, 1974.

Skinner, Hugh. *"Maquinna* Arrived on Time," *Daily Colonist*, December 23, 1975.

Smith, Eve. *Why Port Alice? A History 1917-1965*. Port Alice: self-published, 1980.

Stark, Peter. *Astoria: John Jacob Astor and Thomas Jefferson's Lost Pacific Empire*. New York: HarperCollins, 2015.

Tamm, Eric Enno. *Beyond the Outer Shores: The Untold Odyssey of Ed Ricketts, the Pioneering Ecologist who Inspired John Steinbeck and Joseph Campbell.* Vancouver: Raincoast, 2004.

Turner, Robert D. *The Pacific Princesses: An Illustrated History of Canadian Pacific Railway's Princess Fleet on the Northwest Coast.* Victoria: Sono Nis, 1977.

Turner, Robert D. *Sternwheelers and Steam Tugs: An Illustrated History of the Canadian Pacific Railway's British Columbia Lake and River Service.* Victoria: Sono Nis, 1984.

Turner, Robert D. *Those Beautiful Coastal Liners.* Victoria: Sono Nis, 2001.

Wells, R.E. *There's a Landing Today.* Victoria: Sono Nis, 1988.

West Coast Development Co. brochure, 1913. Victoria: BC Archives, call number NW 971.24 W522.

Young, David Esson. *The Uchuck Years.* Madeira Park: Harbour Publishing, 2012.

INDEX

Note: Page numbers in **bold** refer to photographs or illustrations.

Abraham, Dorothy, 103, 136-37, 213
Ahousaht, 117-19, 121
Alaska, 27, 62, 177
Alberni Canal, 76, 79, 81, 83
Alberni Inlet, 76, 83-84
   See also Alberni Canal
Alcatraz, 70
All Red Line (cable telegraph network), 69, **70**, 72
   See also under Bamfield
American Midwest
   See Midwesterners (students)
Amphitrite Point, 94
Anderson, Maquinna, 24
Arellanes, Lester, 170-71
Arnet, Bjarne, 194
Atleo, Richard, 117

Bamfield, 41, 70-71, 73, **74**, 107
   Trans-Pacific Cable Station, 69-**70**-74, 76
   See also Graveyard of the Pacific
Banfield, William "Eddy," 71
Barkley Sound, 71, 177

BC Ferries Corporation, 213-14
BC Marine Railway Company, 11, 25, 27
   See also Bullen's yard
BC Packers fish plants, 79, 84, 87
Beaver, SS, 13
Beere, Nan, 28-29
Belleville Street terminal
   See Victoria
Blair, John, 89
Bligh Island, 133
Bloedel, Stewart and Welch (pulp and paper mill), 82
Bloom, Alder, 84, 89, 101-2, 121, 138, 140-41
Botanical Beach, 34
Brabant, Augustin, 129, 135
British Empire, 69, 72
Brodie, H.W., 32, 88, 117-18, 134-36, 151, 169, 180, 182
Bullen, Mrs. Fitzherbert, 21-22
Bullen's yard, 11, 20, **21**, 208
   See also BC Marine Railway Company
Bungalow Inn, 51
Burrard Inlet, 82

Cachalot whaling station, 88, 150–51,
152
Canadian Pacific Navigation Company
(CPNC), 13–17, 62
Canadian Pacific Railway Company
(CPR), 15–17, 83–84, 195–96,
200–202, 204, 206, 211, 213
Sunset Cruises, **178–79**, 180, **181**,
182
Canadian Pacific Steamship Company
(CPSC), 63
Cape Beale, 65
Carelmapu, 97–**99**–101
Carmanah Point Lighthouse, 45–46,
63–64
Catface Mountain, 117
Ceepeecee pilchard cannery
See under pilchards
Chief Napoleon Maquinna
See Mowachaht people
Chinese workers, 71–72, 80, 135
Christie Roman Catholic Indian
Residential School, 26, 112–14,
114, 117, 129
Clarke, Ivan, 125–26
Clarke, Mabel, 126
Clayoquot (village), 108–9, **109**
Clayoquot Sound, 77, 108, 111
logging protests (1993), 177
Clo-oose, 45–46, 50, **54**, 189, 204
settlers, **48**, 48–**52**–53
See also Newitt, Angela
See also under Ditidaht people
coal, 84–85
Coal Harbour, 160, 190
Columbia and Kootenay Navigation
Company, 16
Cook, James, 133–34, 136–37

Daykin, W.P., 46
deck class, 115–**16**, 180
Department of Marine and Fisheries,
40–41, 43
Department of National Defence, 31
Desolmes, Fernando, 97, 100
Diez, Rodrigo, 100–101
Ditidaht people, 46, 58–59
canoes, 53–55
Dominion Life Saving Trail, 39, 41, 43
See also West Coast Trail
Dunsmuir, James, 31

Empress ships, 17
Esperanza Inlet, 150
Esperanza Mission Hospital, 143
Esquimalt Harbour, 11, 21
Estevan Point Lighthouse, 130–**131**–32,
153, 193–95
Evans, John, 63–64

Fleming, Sandford, 69, 72
Fraser, George, 89–90, **91**, 93
Fraser River, 13, 187
Friendly Cove
See Yuquot

Gap, the, 57–59
Gibson, Gordon, 194–95
Gibson, Ken, 107–8, **215**
Gibson family, 118–19, 121, 140–41,
151, 160
Gillam, Edward, 19–20, 32–33, **33**, **62**,
98–101, 114, 149, 160, 164, 183–86
Tees, SS, 152–53, 173
Gowlland Rocks, 99–100
Graveyard of the Pacific, 39
Guppy, Tony, 81, 183

gyppo (logging operations), 138-**139**-40

Hamilton, Mike, 28, 77
Hatley Castle, 31
Hernández, Juan Josef Pérez, 127
Hesquiaht (village), 126-27, **127**
Hesquiaht people, 128-29, 131
Holberg, 162-63
Hole-in-the-Wall (bay), 59
Hot Springs Cove
    See Refuge Cove
Hudson's Bay Company, 12-13
Huu-ay-aht people, 71, 73

Indian Chief Copper Mine, **122**, 122-23
Indigenous travellers, 115-16, **116**
Irving, John, 14-15

Japanese fishers, 89, 108
Japanese navy attacks in World War II, 94, 130-31, 160, 189-90, 194
Japanese people, internment in World War II, 131, 192-93
Japanese travellers, 10
John Bright trials
    See Hesquiaht people
Jones, Ray, 95

Kains Island Lighthouse, 155
Kelly, Earle, 112, **113**
Kildonan, 79-80
Kildonan Cannery, **80**
Kinney, C.P., 99
Klondike Gold Rush, 14-15
Kwakiutl women, 157, **158**
Kyuquot (village), 206
Kyuquot Sound, 150

Laurier, Wilfrid, 48
Leeson, Ben, 157
Leeson, Jobe "Joseph," 156
Logan, Ernest, 58
Logan, John, 43
Long Beach, 93-94, 101-2
    See also Matterson, Basil; Matterson, Mary
Longstaff, Frederick, 22, 29-30
Lorraine, MV, 199-200
Lummi Bay Cannery, 53, 58
Lutes, Dal, 141

McCannel, Margery "Madge," **105**
McKay, James Budge, 70
MacKinnon, Martin, 186, **187**, 208
MacLeod, Ron, 104-5
Maquinna, Chief Napoleon
    See Mowachaht people
Maquinna Marine Provincial Park, 126
Mason, J., 20
Masunda, SS, 83-84
Matterson, Basil, **92**, 93
    See also Long Beach
Matterson, Mary, **92**, 93
    See also Long Beach
Maude, SS, 13-14
Meares, John, 135
Midwesterners (students), 34-35
Minnesota Seaside Station, 34-35
Monk, Monteith and Co. Ltd., 48-49
Monks, Harold, **102**, **105**, 193
Monks, Katie, 193
Moore, Bill, 157-59
Moser, Charles, 114, 117, 137
Mosquito Harbour, 108
Mowachaht people, 133-34
    Chief Napoleon Maquinna, 22, 133-34, 136-37

Neroutsos, Cyril D., 182
Newitt, Angela, 51, 53
Nitinat Lake channel
   See Gap, the
Nogi (Great Dane), 100
Nootka (village), **135**, 135-37
Nootka Cannery, 137, **137**
Nootka Convention of 1790, 134
Nootka Sound, 133-34
Noronic, SS, 200
Nuu-cha-nulth people, 2, 125

Pachena Lighthouse, 61
Pachena Point, 41
Pacific Coast Steamship Company
   (California), 62, 177
Palmer, Melville, 209
Pass of Metford, 94
Peterson, Jan, 63, 73-74
pilchards, 77-79
   Ceepeecee pilchard cannery,
      141-**142**-43
   reduction plants, 78-80, 87, 119
   See also BC Packers fish plants
Port Alberni, 81-83
Port Alice, 164-65
Port Alice Pulp Mill, **165**
Port Gillam, 116
Port Renfrew, 33-34
   See also Graveyard of the Pacific
Port San Juan
   See Port Renfrew
Princess Maquinna, SS, **21**-22, 25-26, **28**,
   30, **47**, **54**, **62**, **65**, **74**, **93**, **105**, **120**,
   122, **137**, **142**, **161**, **166**, **207**, **208**,
   208-9, 211-13
   boilers, 201-**203**-6
   construction, 19-**21**-24
   crew, **106**, **187**
   layout, 23, **24**

   meals, 35-37, 60-61
   passengers, 31-32, **62**, **102**, **116**
   World War II, **192**, 195-97
Princess Norah, SS, 36, **36**, **181**, 182-83,
   184, 213

Quantrill, William
   See Sharp, John
Quatsino (village), 159-60, **161**
Quatsino Sound, 159, 166
Queen City, SS, 14-15, 34

Race Rocks Lighthouse, 31
radio, 111-12
   See also Kelly, Earle
Rae-Arthur, Ada Annie, 129-30
Rattenbury, Francis Mawson, 7, 69-70
Refuge Cove, 125-26
Resolution Cove, 133
Ricketts, Ed, 164-65, 169-70
Rivers Inlet, 115-16, 167
Robertson, Neil, 109
Ronning, Bernt, 162-63
Royal Roads Military College
   See Hatley Castle

Sadler, Catherine, 155-56
Sadler, James, 155-56
Santiago, 127
Scott, Bruce, 71-72, 74-76
Scott, Pauline, 74-75
sea otter fur trade, 103, 127, 134-35
Sechart whaling station, 87-88, **88**
Sharp, John, 160-62
Shaughnessy, Thomas, 20, 22
Shipwrecked Mariner's Trail
   See Dominion Life Saving Trail
Skinner, Hugh, 146-48
Smith, Adam, 28
Solander Island, 155

southern route, 169–70, 174–75
  fog, 171–74
Sparrowhawk, HMS, 128–29
Stamp, Edward, 81–82
Strait of Juan de Fuca, 31, 40

Tahsis, 138, 140–41
Taku, **208**, 209
Tees, SS, 14–15, **15**, 27–29, 34, 50, 62–63, 108
  See also under Gillam, Edward
Thompson, Robert "Red," 64–66, 75, 83, 186, **187**
Thompson, William "Black," 83, 186
Tilden, Josephine, 35
Tla-o-qui-aht people, 103–4
Tofino, 103–9, 190
Tofino Inlet, 108–9
Tonquin, 103
Trans-Pacific Cable Station
  See All Red Line
  See also under Bamfield
Troup, James W., 16–18, 19–20, 25–27, 29, 32, 62, 182
Tsusiat Falls, 59–60, **60**

Uchuck III, 214
Uchucklesaht, 79–80, **80**
Ucluelet, 89–90, **93**, 94, 190
University of Minnesota, 35

Valencia, SS, 41, 6
Vancouver, 82
Vargas Island, 116
Veta C, 206
Victoria, 89, 175
  Belleville Street terminal, **8**, 25, 205, 214

Walbran, John T., 22
Walters Cove, 154
Warren, Margaret, 188
West Coast Development Company, 49–50
  brochures, **49**
West Coast Trail, 39, 41, **42**, 43, 59
wharves (west coast), 26–27
Willapa, SS, 14–15
Wingen, Bob, 61, 66, 106–7
Wingen, Hilmar, 105–6
Winter Harbour, 156–57
Winter Harbour Canning Company
  See Leeson, Jobe "Joseph"
World War I, 51, 53, 116, 189
World War II, **93**, 94, 189-**191**-**192**-93, 197
  See also Estevan Point Lighthouse;
  Japanese people, internment in
  World War II; Japanese navy
  attacks in World War II; *Princess
  Maquinna*, SS
Wouwer, Johnnie Vanden, 9, 72, 79, 94–95, 107, 188
Wright, "Shorty," 9, 106, **106**, 130, 165

Young, David, 150, 172, 188
Yuquot, 133–35, **135**
  graveyard, 135–36

Zeballos, 145-**146**-49
Zeballos Inlet, 145